Simply
Five Energy fields

(A collection of essays on Earth, Water, Fire, Air and Space)

By

Swami Nityamuktananda Saraswati

Published by: 5 Elements
Global Ltd

Offered to

The One that unfolds as the Many

'Come forth into the light of things,
Let nature be your teacher'
(William Wordsworth)

If only we could understand the songs of birds, if only we could interpret the pattern of clouds, if only we could tune into the whispers of stones and the songs of the waves, we would not need books. But as we can't, we need help to understand life and ourselves. To truly understand, we need guidance and grace. I would like to offer this book, with immense gratitude, at the feet of my Gurus from whom I receive both.

Foreword and Acknowledgement

'Ancient people in all parts of the world have been aware of nature. They were not distracted by Bingo halls, shopping malls and Televisions, but spent time to feel the solid earth underneath their feet, to watch the flowing river; to feel the warmth of a living fire and understand the importance of the light of the sun; they felt the touch of the breeze on their skin and they watched the vast open spaces above. They experienced and learned……they became aware that each of their senses is finely tuned to one of these natural phenomena. And these phenomena have similarity and influence as to what happens in their own body and life.' They called these elemental forces Earth, Water, Fire, Air and Space.

Nothing has changed in this perspective; today we might call these forces: Gravity, Fluidity, electro-dynamic waves, Symmetry and consciousness or any amount of other base building blocks. What remains the same however is their essential characteristics and how they are related to weave the web of life and our total interconnectedness with these.

The tragedy in our times is that much of the vast body of gathered knowledge about these natural forces seems to be disappearing, just as hundreds and thousands of living species of plant and animal kingdom disappear, as many languages disappear and as whole indigenous cultures disappear. Why, because not only have we become global (even globally destructive), but also greedy and materialistic…We have lost the perspective of understanding ourselves in the context as these forces, which leads to the banes of our time: environmental pollution and human suffering. We lost the sense of who we are in the Movement of Life. I hope this book will stimulate the reader to rediscover some interconnectedness within

Nature and that She will help us back to health and wholeness.

The material presented here, are articles that have first been made available as monthly contributions in a newsletter. They have their starting point in Yogic thinking, however not in any narrow sense, but in true yogic spirit, as universal perspective.

I would like to thank all those who helped to make these articles into a book, especially my publisher Barbara Murrell, for her tireless co-operation. And Laura Calletti for allowing me to use her beautiful photographs. (lauracalletti@gmail.com). Thanks to Justin Goode for his photograph on page 148.

Contents

Introduction

The Five Elements, a universal concept.

This topic is especially relevant to Yoga; understood as the science of 'stilling the modifications of the mind' (*chitta vritti nirodhana)* with the goal of returning to our original nature.
However: How can we reach this stillness, this peace of mind? How comes our mind is so fickle and disturbed? How do these disturbances rise in body and mind? How can I find peace? What is 'my original nature'?

To find answers to these questions, in one way or another has been the endeavour of just about any culture and time, consequently the Five Element concept has become a vast subject, timelessly spanning the globe. In our times, we find even common ground with the most modern branch of science; Quantum theory. The Five Element concept is alive, describing the timeless wisdom of the Movement of Life!
Let's have a wee glimpse and see what we can learn from it.

Ancient people in all parts of the world have been aware of nature. They were not distracted by Bingo halls and Televisions, but spent time to feel the solid earth underneath their feet, to watch the flowing river; to feel the warmth of a living fire and understand the importance of the light of the sun; they felt the touch of the breeze on their skin and they watched the vast open spaces above. They experienced and learned……they became aware that each of their senses is finely tuned to one of these natural phenomena. And these phenomena have similarity and influence as to what happens in their own body and life.

As much as ten-thousand years ago or more people started to

try to influence these powers and gradually made them into Gods; to worship, pacify or manipulate. They humanised the elements and coloured them with their culturally conditioned minds, which in time unfortunately fed the muddy pool of religious differences. (But let's keep that aside.)

Man's experience with the elemental forces revealed an inherent hierarchy within them; Earth is less fluid than Water, Fire less tangible than Water, Air is less observable than Fire- and Space just about escapes all together. In this way Space, the most subtle begged the question of whether it is still of this world? Furthermore: is it an element or is it the root of all the others? Thus Space becomes linked with the idea of the original cause of existence. We exist within this Space. We too are made up of the Five Elements as the Bhagavad Gita (Chapter XVII/15) points out: 'whatever action man performs by his body, speech and mind - whether right, or the reverse - these Five are its causes…'

Man experienced himself and his world as a manifestation of the Five Elements. He understood them as the material cause, yet as Space holds all the Elements there must be a subtler cause where physical Space itself is held, another Space, another dimension.

Observation, reasoning and meditation led earliest mankind to this 'subtle Space' – he called it by various names: The Absolute, God, IO Maori); Biami (Australian Aboriginals) Jok (Africa)
The Tao (China), the Cosmic Christ (medieval Europe) or simply 'consciousness Space' (chidakasha) ancient India; the latter as any of the named cultures has many names for this 'beyond'…such as 'Brahman Nirguna' (without form) – or Parasiva or '*Sadasiva* who shines as the self-resplendent light bringing forth the five great

elements…' So says Swami Sivananda of Rishikesh. Shiva itself is present in all elements, as there is nothing on earth that is not his expression; so we all share this dual nature…physicality and divinely, as matter and what lies beyond matter, what in-spires matter.

Albert Einstein's famous formula: $E=mc^2$ made us aware, that matter has another dimension i.e. energy - but few know that he indicated that both these have a common source in the 'Greatest Unknowable Mystery' i.e. the Absolute, without form indeed described by the American Indians as Great Mystery (Wakan Takan), who expresses in the phenomenal world as energy and matter.

Using 'element-speak' we could say: the Absolute Space of consciousness (some call it Shiva) and his action power (some call it Shakti) together weave that, which 'solidifies energy into matter', much like milk is churned into butter. There is much written since time began how these two powers are knitted together, let's leave that aside and focus on the matter aspect; because there is almost unanimous agreement, that what we as human can perceive through our senses is this matter aspect, we call the phenomenal existence or: Creation. In Yoga this is called **Prakriti (***Prakriti, Maya, Shakti or simply 'creative energy') there are many names for HER across the globe* (call it what you may). The perception of it is shared by all people because ,one could say: we have five sense organs in order to perceive five 'fields of energy, vibrating at five frequency bands, the most gross forms of these we call Earth, Water, Fire, Air and physical Space.' Then the question comes, how does abstract energy become a tree, or me?

The Yogic teaching, not far from other traditions is, that Consciousness (Latin: con-science; with knowledge) and energy come together and through their interaction change it to ever denser material in a multiplicity of forms. We could say there are three things involved: intelligence (wisdom), interaction (transforming power) and the manifest result (objects). These three we recognize in Yoga as the three Gunas: *sattva, rajas, and tamas.* These three subtle versions of energy, (you might like to explore each in great depth) continue to interact, permanently moving, creating the next layer of perceptible manifestation.

In this way pure sattva is **Space**; the interaction between sattva and rajas creates movement we experience as **Air**. Rajas by itself, as continuous 'action power' is **Fire**; action power in matter, creates fluidity, we call **Water**; and matter in a stable state we call Earth. You can see that the scheme is dynamic – not limited to the simplified understanding of words like 'Water' (as simply something that comes out of the tap.)

In Indian thought, it is furthermore thought that these different states **come into being through <u>intent</u>.** One portrays consciousness behind the apparent universe as a cosmic Persona, with supreme intelligence and will. (Quantum theorists prefer to say: knowledge riding on energy like a jockey on the back of a racehorse.) Whatever images minds use - this intelligence creates conditions which result (in the obedience of the 'horse') - in actions with intent.

If that Absolute 'Being' intends to experience sound, it creates space in which sound can travel; if *IT* intends to experience touch, air is created, unseen and subtle. Wishing to see, this cosmic person brings fire into being, and this fire expands into the numerous sources of light. Intending to experience taste, as well as coolness to counteract fire, water comes into being. And lastly, by its mere wish to smell, earth with its faculty of smell comes into being. --- (In this way wisdom 'wears the dress of a cosmic being'/ similar versions, we find across the globe, even though sometimes with less detail).

This means the world is willed i.e. ideation or thought precedes word on the journey into existence. This is noteworthy; it goes one step deeper than in most cultures, where the world comes into existence through the spoken word. Here the idea precedes and, is the seed that grows into the word, by the power of ***Matrika-shakti,*** (prime expression of the very creative energy, we mentioned above). Sacred words in India are called mantra. One of the most ancient mantras is: *Ohm namah Shivaya*; these syllables stand for: *na* - earth, *ma* - water, *shi* - fire, *va* - air, *ya* - space. This mantra embodies the Five Elements.

Of course man also consists of these Five Elements which dissolve in death, as we know from the **Tibetan Book of the Dead** and ...common sense: the bodies flesh is earthy, so it returns to the earth. Blood etc. are liquid and they return to the water-element. The fire (heat) and the light in the body belong to the fire-element, they return to it. The air is offered to the cosmic air. Space merges into space... Furthermore earth dissolves in water, water in fire, fire in air and air in space. Space should be merged with cosmic space, which is the cause.

Again and again, Space comes out as something special... we have to keep this in mind; because Space itself is pregnant with the intelligence, the consciousness that is responsible for generating form out of the Five Elements. Meaning: although the forms dissolve, Space energy holds the accumulated knowledge, or mind stuff of the person! Has it enough coherence it will re-incarnate… take form again!

Space in its dual aspect, as physical-holding physical form (akasha), and as potential, knowledge of absolute abstraction (Chidakasha)…stands out not only in Indian thought; universally this Fifth Element (without properties) is considered the divine door; (it is quint-essential) the awareness of this non-physical 'Space' is a door…(dharana) through which illumination happens, through which we become aware of our true Nature.

A story told about Sankaracharya (a supreme influential philosopher in India, much like Plato in the Western hemisphere) might serve to illustrate: It is said that when he was a young man, he went in search of his teacher. After traveling a long distance, he arrived tired at a hermitage; he walked three times around it then was directed to the cave where Govindapada lived; he prostrated at his door and began to chant a hymn in praise of the sage, then continued. 'Praying to Thee for instruction in the truth of Brahman, I salute Thee, the repository of all great virtues!'

Praised thus, the sage came out of his super-consciousness state, and asked, 'who are you?' In reply Sankara said the following, indicative of his great spiritual enlightenment: 'Revered Sir, I am neither the earth, nor water, nor fire, nor air, nor sky, nor any of their properties. I am not the senses and the mind even. I am Shiva, the division-less essence of Consciousness.' Hearing these words, the sage was delighted…

All over the globe, but in our times especially in Asia these concepts have been explored and applied in various disciplines such as Ayurveda, TCM (Traditional Chinese Medicine), Shiatsu and Yoga. Ayurveda for example is built on the understanding of the five Elements, and that not in a purely literal fashion but (just as in China) in innumerable levels of subtle associations; each communicating the inherent principle of the Element – for the benefit of re-balancing people and their lives. In this way **Air** is seen as transparent, a rarefied, kinetic force which sets the created in motion. By **Fire** is meant the force in nature that by transforming one-into-another…produces heat and radiates light. By **Water** we understand the cohesive aspect of reality which holds things together, perfectly and simply, even if "so unlikely "as two gases making the ubiquitous H_20 molecule. **Earth** is understood to be the final solid (difficult to change) result and **Space** is understood as the prototype of complex generative subtle form.

Together, the Five Elements are **expressions of the life-energy called *Prana*, (Ch/Ki etc.)** flowing through the body like electricity in different currents, in channels (Meridians/ Nadis).

They build, nourish and maintain physical organs: Earth energy is linked to the stomach and spleen; Water energy is linked to bladder and kidney; Fire energy to heart, small intestines; metabolism and the immune system. The Air Element is linked to Lung and Large intestines; Space energy is linked to Liver and Gallbladder. When there is imbalance in either of the energy currents, it affects our life-force and imbalance produces eventually 'dis-ease.' Balance is Health and Peace of Mind!

Imbalance or biological decay – is brought about by conditions called *doshas* (meaning 'that which darkens'). Each *dosha* receives its characteristics from particular elements. Thus the *dosha* called *Vata* reflects disharmony in Space and Air; *Pitta* reflects disturbances in Fire, (some say Fire and Water); *Kapha* reflects on Water and Earth.

The particular combination of energies (mixture of Elements) present when we enter this world at birth, is known as our 'innate constitution' or *prakruti.* So we ourselves are shaped by these Five aggregates; their mixture determines our physical and mental wellbeing …and character! The latter led to a universal typology (resonating in Jung's psychology). As they affect our minds, they shape 'the modifications of the mind' and with it how we experience the world. Balancing the Elements balances the Mind!

As everything that we perceive is made up **of these energy fields…**, their effects can be and is observed and used in countless ways, in many cultures. Most prevalent in **medicine, yes but also in music, art, architecture, astrology, yoga (asana) and even to govern and settle disputes.** So far I used mainly Indian and Yogic phraseology – but as mentioned before, the concept is universal. Let's look at some others:

The Vietnamese monk, the Venerable Thich Nhat Hahn, has Buddha himself explain the teachings of the Five Elements (Old path white clouds): "The Buddha understood that Rahula was ripe to receive certain teachings. He said: 'Rahula, learn from the earth. Whether people spread pure and fragrant flowers, perfume, or fresh milk on it, or discard filthy foul-smelling faeces, urine, blood, mucus and spit on it, the earth receives it all equally without clinging or aversion. When pleasant or unpleasant thoughts arise, don't let them entangle or enslave you... Learn from the water, Rahula. When people wash dirty things in it, the water is not sad or disdainful. Learn from Fire. Fire burns all things without discrimination. It is not ashamed to burn impure substances. Learn from the air. The air carries all fragrances whether sweet or foul. Rahula practice loving-kindness to overcome anger... Practice compassion to overcome cruelty... Practice non-attachment to overcome prejudice. Non-attachment is the way of looking at all things openly and equally. This is because that is. That is because this is. Myself and others are not separate. Do not reject one thing only to chase after another." The all-encompassing detachment of Space is unmistakably represented.

As **Buddhism** spread there was a melting pot of knowledge from India and China. The Elements were a distinct part of this; understood as states of being (*skandas* or aggregates); analysed in terms of four gross elements (solidity, fluidity, heat and motion and their derivatives; the fifth being reserved for mind/consciousness). The **Tibetan** Cosmology reveals there integration: 'In the First Round of our Planet, one element alone - Fire was evolved. In the fire-mist... cosmos assumed a rotary motion and became a blazing globular body of undifferentiated primeval forces, all other elements lay in embryo... In the second Round, as the Element Fire assumed definite form, the Element Air separated from it and enwrapped the embryonic Planet as a shell covers an egg... In the Third Round, as the Planet, bathed in the Element Air and fanned by it, abated its fiery nature, the Element Water came forth from the vaporous air... In the Fourth Round, in which the Planet still is, air and water neutralised the activities of their Parent Fire; and the Fire, bringing forth the Element Earth, became encrusted with it.'

As we heard: Tibetan- , Chinese- and Ayurvedic Medicine all are built on the Five Elements (slight difference usually turn out to be in name only!) Some of these shared attributes are: stubbornness, arrogance/obduracy as well as equanimity are linked to the **Earth** Element and frustration/aggression as well as clarity/insight to the **Water** element. The indiscriminate and obsessive consuming nature is related to **Fire,** as well as discriminating awareness/ compassion. Paranoia is linked to **Air** as well as confidence/ability and self-accomplishment. Torpor and confusion is linked to Space as well as ubiquitous intelligence and pervasive awareness and spiritual achievement.

In Japan all the above is shared (see application in Shiatsu) but the most important contribution here is the role they play in all the Zen Arts.

The Absolute **in Chinese** culture is called the TAO (in **Korea** – Taiji); this Indescribable expresses and moves between two poles. Hence we have Yin (qui) and Yang (li) and the Movement in between--- see the three Gunas? These are the instigator of all change which then unfolds and **is** 'broken down into tangible components… the five elements' or ***wu-hsing*** penetrating Chinese Culture from earliest times to now.

Beyond Asia we find rich pickings too, if we are able to leave our overly left-brained mind, and include myth and legends of Aboriginal **Australia and Africa.** Here people lived continuously in the awareness of being one with nature. Australians refer to this state of being - as 'Dreaming'. As nomads, they were moving freely within both 'Spaces'; in continuous awareness of ancestors and the Father of Fathers, *Bai-a-mi.* Life was/is truly holistic. The experience of the Five Elements was/is an integral, sacred part of life; which finds expression in numerous legends and myth about the Elements in the guise of Dream-heroes. There is *Kanbi* and *Jitabid* for Fire; the Water Element appears as *Tilak, the frog; Ankotarinja* and/or *Kunappipi (the earth-womb)* as different aspects of Earth; Geeger–Geeger is a Wind or Air representative and so on, and so on.

In tribal **Africa** the Elements are understood as the multifaceted expression of one spirit force, *JOK* a divine energy that lives in trees, animals, people, mountains and rivers alike. In our time Malidoma Patrice Somé, shaman and scholar shares his wisdom of the Dagara of Burkina Faso, by relating that not only the cosmological cycle is based on the Elements, but village structures, the judicary system, naming ceremonies, people and …even cultures carry the characteristics of the Five Elements…….

Some of the same applications we find **in the Americas**. The Medicine Wheel and the Twenty Count are both of immense importance in the world of the original Inhabitants!

In Meso- and South America we find detailed knowledge of the Five Elements enshrined in the ancient language called *Nahuatl;* rich in symbolism and wisdom. Life and eons of time were understood as cycles of the elements. The kingdom of the Incas was known as 'the Four-Corner-Region' and is reputed to be built by Patchikoto, on the principle of co-operation and harmony between all Elements as key to the idea of the 'Fifth Sun Age' (in order to prevent a major cataclysm). Here (long before Christianity) the symbolism of the cross is used to represent the Five Elements: It has the ascending line of fire and water, the movement line from left to right, for spirit to matter (Air and Earth) they meet in the centre Space as 'the fifth dimension.'

What about **Europe**? (There is much to say about early Europe and the Celtic wisdom, but let's begin with the origin of present European culture, which can be said to lie in Greece. Plotinus (and many before him) talked quiet specific of the Elements: 'Earth ... the very sea... the great air...the ether and the far spread heavens... permeated by supreme pure Intelligence streaming throughout existence, as though 'from all sides pouring in its light'. Earth, Water, Fire, Air and Space have their 'indwelling principles and Spirit Soul'. But with Aristoteles (384-322 BC) this world-view changed; the Fifth, more spiritual Element (Space of 'indwelling spirit') disappears from the agenda- which gets limited to the four more material, gross Elements. With that the materialistic thinking, which finds its crowning glory in today's world started!

From then on, mainstream Europe recognized only Four Elements. But somehow it could never totally suppress the Fifth. There were always some which worked with the Five: such as the Christian Mystics; i.e. For Fr.M.D.Chenu and his better known contemporary Hildegard von Bingen (12th.century) the Cosmic Christ became the all-pervading spiritual Fifth Element, in which all existed and which existed in all.

Hildegard von Bingen , German Abbess from the Rhine-valley; was an inspired theological scholar, composer of music and an artist, who wove the Five Elements into all her work, from her famous *mandalas/ illuminations* to her impressive work as medical doctor. Her book 'Causae et curae' is entirely working with the Five Elements 'These basic elements are within themselves so interconnected, that none can be separated from the other, and they hold so tightly together, that one calls them the essential structure of the universe….all our deeds touch and concern the Elements and are in turn touched by these' · She took the natural forces as her teacher and wrote: '**Fire** is the highest power under the heavens …. responsible for the red blood, body-temperature; the light of vision etc. **Water**…nourishes all things as wetness…water...manifests as juice in the process of fertility… **Earth** has a stabilizing effect… she lets things grow out of herself…supports all creatures… is in the flesh and the cells of bones …in its ability to reproduce… ." Consider that this is 12th century Europe, three hundred years before the first anatomy book on 'the working of the body' (Andreas Vesalius) - and it is in accord with ancient medicine systems in China and India!

In the Renaissance painters, poets and ordinary people rediscovered the lushness of nature and the notion of the Five Elements came back. It was fertile ground on which holistic thinking could eventually re-grow, and prepare the ground for what we call today complementary medicine.

So basically the world over people and throughout time, agree:

Earth is the most dense – the state of solidity – we can perceive with all five senses.

Water is less so – the state of fluidity – we can perceive by four senses. (No smell)

Fire is constant transformation, constant action- we can perceive by three senses –i.e. less considerable less dense - (no taste, no touch)

Air is movement, subtle transparent movement – we can perceive only with two senses (no taste, no smell, no vision)

Space still subtler, nearly imperceptible; we perceive it through sound alone. Yet despite containing all others, it remains untouched by their movement, ever calm ever in balance.

These manifestations – are recognisable in the entire Universe, as well as in our body. (Earth -stomach and the spleen! Water - kidney and bladder! Fire - heart and small intestines! Air - lung and large intestines! Space - liver and gallbladder) Blocks in the energy flow to these (be it on the physical, mental or spiritual level) give congestion, pain – restlessness of the mind and - eventually illness. For us to be healthy and have a peaceful mind the blocks and their resulting toxicity has to be removed; for that Yoga prescribes asana. Each of us has individual blocks in our energy system. To know these blocks – to remove these blocks with discrimination – is to walk the spiritual path, which includes choosing the right process of purification (i.e. Yoga practice!) There is much more to explore….

Spiritual Dimensions of the Elements

We have learned that in the known universe there are five fields of energy, that we term the FIVE ELEMENTS. Everything, including ourselves is made of these fields of energy. As we heard, each being is dominated by one Element, giving the body and personality its 'flavour' and accordingly shows the strength and weakness of the individual. Yoga, Tantra, Ayurveda, TCM, and other complementary medicines work with this. The five Elements play an important role in self-discovering, balancing the personality and working on the mind.

The particularities of each Element shape our path through life (whether we are aware of it or not). Studying these energies helps us to understand ourselves. It helps also to understand our path in life; meaning the life journey we make. An acorn can only evolve into an oak tree, however whether it evolves into weak crooked one, or a mighty old one is – to some extent "up to itself". This individual unfolding on and within a path, in Yoga we call 'dharma'; this **dharma shapes our spiritual path.**

Let's look at the Elements from this angle. Wisdom teachers all over the globe, mystics and recent scientist agree that the universe is made out of conscious or intelligent energy. Energy vibrates; we can measure and observe it.

We know, that the Five Elements represent five groups or frequency ranges varying from relative low (Earth) to relatively high frequencies (Space). Each group has many associations and relations. Whether you talk about a colour, body- tissues or emotions of Earth they all share a similar range or spectrum.

Now, you know when your car makes a funny sound, it vibrates and the sound of that vibration is disturbing to us and we worry whether there is something wrong … and take it to the garage to put it right!

Being in harmony with our body and the world, is vibrating in tune with the Orchestra of life!

As we have seen previously, there is one range of frequency that is 'greater/higher' hence containing all other; yet is not influenced or changed by them…i.e. Space. The Yogic scriptures have two words for Space (akasha and chidakasha). Normally when we speak of Space, we refer to that one which is part of the manifesting Elements and holds them creatively in itself. The second word for Space refers to something Absolute-which has no attributes, no form of any kind, can't be described ...not even by our simile of vibrating energy. It is 'other', is the Indescribable; or even God.
Every cell of our body holds much of the former version of Space, hence we say: we are mainly Space. This Space-energy is metabolized in the Throat Chakra (esoteric Anatomy knows of 7 or even 12 such transformers). Beyond the Throat Chakra are two further levels, these relate to the higher, indescribable, un-manifest Space.

So when we talk about Elements having an illuminating, spiritual role for our life-path, we look at those energies working up to and incl. the throat Chakra.

Elements play a particular role, in the development of man. Evolution takes place from the subtle to the gross and the gross to the subtle. The spiritual path, is that path on which we learn the lessons from the gross body, the most solid Element (Earth) - to the most subtle Element, i.e. Space - and beyond (working solely with Space is going into the realm that Patanjali (author of the Yoga Sutras) describes amongst the Yogic powers; because just as Space holds the other four elements, so the Yogi who lives entirely in this realm has the skill and knowledge to hold and manipulate the other four Elements). We are far from that level; our goal is to learn the lessons the manifest world has to offer. We recognize however two distinct phases:

1) to learn the lessons of the Elements and balance them within the Space Element (i.e. sattva guna/ throat –Chakra).

2) and to ascend beyond the physical, altogether; (while still in this body it means working with the Ajna chakra and the Sahasra.)

Each step has its merits, each step is necessary, we can't jump class. (A primary school student is equal to a university student. Yet he cannot understand the lectures of the Nuclear Scientist. So, be aware, when we talk about the spiritual lessons of the Five Elements, it is lessons to be learned in the manifest world which is perceived and shaped entirely by our mind. We perceive existence only through the mind, so this instrument ... needs to be fine-tuned. Right understanding here, can save much time and effort.

The ancient founding Masters of yoga science therefore engaged into self-inquiry. They founded Yoga as a science of the mind. They might ask us:

'When you created a spaceship, the metal and machinery converted into the spaceship has made progress, has changed, through the touch of human intelligence. When you can flash a light on or off, the light has made progress through the touch of human ingenuity. No doubt... the material world has made progress.

But what progress, human being, have you made in the past 5000 years?

If you were left in the desert or cave without any props ...if you stood absolutely naked in solitude... what could you do with your six foot –frame?
In what way have you evolved, improved on what the man 5000 years ago could do?
...Can you, through application of your wisdom and mental ability turn an opponent's anger into peace....? Can you indeed control your own anger?
Can you pull yourself out of your own depression (without paying someone)? Can you slow down your breath and prolong your life? Can you improve your digestion or permit greater absorption of oxygen into your system? Can you at will produce antidotes to poisons and pollutions that your own society produces?
Can you raise your own body temperature at will; heal your own cell regeneration from a cancerous assault?'(Meditation and Mantra; Swami Veda Bharati; Himalaya Institute 1981)

All these are things true Yogis can do, because all these functions depend on the mind... and control of the mind...is the key! Modern man changes his/her environment to suit themselves; the Yogi changes himself, so he can live anywhere happily. This is true evolution of the human kind. We all are far away from that goal, I only mention it to paint the picture of how the path, we call spiritual path is actually a necessity for human evolution.
We start with the simple stuff! Learning from the obvious, observable Elements around us, what are these lessons?
Remember: the declared goal of Yoga (Patanjali) is to 'return to our original nature!'

And what is that? All wise teachers from Buddha to Christ, from Mohammed to the Dalai Lamas, from Shamans to therapists and psychologists, Rishis and Yogis agree the essential question is: **Who are you?**

The African Shaman Malidoma Patrica Some writes: 'The centre is both within and without.
It is everywhere. But we must realise it exists, find it, and be with it, for without the centre we cannot tell who we are, where we come from and where we are going.'

The American Indians tell us we need to find our own drumbeat inside ourselves, the rhythm of Life that is specific to ourselves, yet fits totally into the drumbeat of mother Earth.

Here we have **<u>the spiritual Path for the Element Earth,</u>** starting the inquiry into who we are. We start by getting to know our body and how it behaves; we become aware of our and others physical existence? This awareness will eventually take us to the knowledge that our body is life –force in its most solid state **in relationship** to all other. The body is life in-carnate (made flesh)! To discover this is a major goal of asana practice. (Health and fitness is a by-product!) Only once we can see, that we are more than apparent body, can we progress to the next level in our *'Sadhana'* (spiritual practice). If we understand ourselves as "body only"… we also seek the divine in that form. Our mind limits what is "out there" according to what it has stored inside itself.

What is the God of a Lion, it's a bigger Lion! For Man to understand God – God has to be seen as man, incarnate in the flesh as Jesus, the son of Mary, the carpenter's son; or Krishna, divine incarnation, dancing with the shepherdesses.

A body orientated mind has to give the Divine a body, a manifest expression. This is the root of image worship. (However *if 'God is everything',* then HE is also in the made statue!!!! But let's leave that….).

The spiritual lesson for Earth to learn then, is that I and the apparent universe am/is more than the form! Everything has a divine core; the inquiry into 'who am I' ultimately has to find this core of Divinity. Seeing that not only in myself, but in others, and effectively in all of creation results in a life of respect and love to all Beings!

What is Water's spiritual path? Water's main characteristic is fluidity. Having become aware of not being limited to this physical body; we are ready to understand that this body/ i.e. matter, constantly changes form. Now a baby, now a man. Now a seed, now a tree. Now alive, now dead. This is the flow of matter. Recognizing of this "shape-shifting", makes us *aware of constant dissolution* *and creation; makes us aware of the ephemeral nature of form.* Nowhere does this show more than in our emotions, we are happy today, sad tomorrow. For a time we are this, for a time we are that!For a time we nourish others, for a time we take from others, for a time we rest!

Focus on the transient *... is the key to sadhana with Water qualities.* Hence the 'Water- person', is preoccupied with the question: where do I come from, where am I going?

Both Earth and Water have the quality of nurturing and supporting. People with Water dominance however, feel into others. They know your plight - can be my plight! Their illness, sorrow, helplessness- can be in the next moment our sorrow, illness etc. 'I am like the rest of humanity, or even the rest of creation. I share suffering and joy in the same as the rest of humanity.' Hence I am willing and able to serve others! Compassion has its root here.

Water's spiritual path is marked by Ahimsa; Respect and Non-violence to all others!

Non-violence is the beginning of a path, which eventually leads to giving up the Ego! Surrendering one's own interest to that of the greater Good/ God/Guru.

This mirrors Water's ability to adapt; every moment Water is aware of needing to change; it's pre-occupation with the question: 'where am I going'.

The fear of the unknown looms large; the fear of losing what I have got, the fear of self-annihilation even, is often present. Sadhana here needs to be supported *by studying the scriptures, or find an authentic teacher - to gain a road-map of where to go.*

However, the desire to adapt, to help others and share (however laudable) is still based on accepting the material, body as paramount. But by taking up so many forms, being so adaptable, having such a rich and varied life...Water learns that any of these roles are not really him/herself.

'I am not limited to any role, emotion or game...tomorrow I might be different! ***If I am not the body, nor its roles, emotions and games ... then ...what am I?'***

The focus of sadhana changes gradually from body-identification - to seeing what else I am, with it changes the object of worship; different forms of the Divine are discovered (now Buddha, now Christ, now Krishna...)

Let's turn to the spiritual path of Fire.

Fire is the most often used symbol for the spiritual path; i.e. one speaks of the Fire of Yoga, the fire of devotion or love, the fire of austerities; the fire of knowledge etc. etc. What does it mean?

Fire is transformation; any one of the above can be used to transform the being. When we are truly loving, truly devoted, we identify with the object of our love and loose ourselves. The result is a different me. This absorption is the key to transformation. It is said, that experiencing the ecstasy of divine revelation has a lasting character-changing effect. Furthermore absorption in Nature, in Beauty … can have a similar effect; subject and object merge into one.

People, who have a dominant Fire Element, are drawn to the path of Devotion. Here we can pray, we can relate to God; just as God relates to his son. There are two forces…in intimate relationship; devoted and the object of devotion, Fire and its burning power!.

Similarly **the *fire of knowledge*** transforms our perception of the world and ourselves so that we clearly see the temporary as unreal and start to search for the real. Insight into the nature of impermanence changes our attachment; we start to understand the interdependence of formless and form, or of Spirit and matter – and thus loose our fixed idea of being a manifest separate entity, instead we melt just like lover and the beloved; worshipped and the object of worship… and experience that there is only One. Through knowledge or devotion, I realize that I am not only body, not only mind…but I am 'other'; be it 'spirit'; even universal spirit..

Hence the Yoga Sutras recommend as a key principal: **Devotion or Ishwara Pranidhara!** The Fire of Devotion and the Fire of Knowledge need to come together; that is the spiritual teaching of Fire! Then we can celebrate, experience the Joy that we are!

Now to **<u>the spiritual path indicated by the Air Element.</u>**
We all know the word prana means Air; but prana also means life force, however the two are directly connected. Hence to practice prana-yama (control of breath) is the most obvious message from the Air Element.

There is a story in the Upanishads, according to which Mind, breath, speech, ear and eye argued amongst themselves, who is the most important. To solve the dispute, they decided one by one to leave the body and asses which one is the least missed.
Speech left… the body, although mute…lived happily on.
The eye left; …the body although blind …lived happily on.
The ear left…. the body, although dumb…. lived happily on.
The mind left…. The body although in coma, lived on.
Once prana left however, the body died and decomposed.

Pranayama no doubt is an important practice; it builds vitality, which is obviously important for doing spiritual practices. But the real strength comes not from the physical activity, but from surrendering to the divine. Pranayama teaches this *thorough* letting-go; the out-breath is vital (without it there is stagnation and congestion in the chest). Furthermore Pranayama goes much beyond the physical, it enables us to gain control over the mind (esp. letting-go). The power that works the mind, we call intellect. And it's the intellect which helps us to penetrate delusion and illusions we have about ourselves, and the world.

To develop discrimination (an intellectual version of letting go) is the spiritual practice the Air Element teaches. Discrimination asks us, what we need to let go of; be it tension via the out-breath, be it outmoded concepts and ideas…of the mind. The Air Element challenges us to let go of the unwanted and sharpen and clarify our perception of reality as it is. Spiritual practice at this point becomes the Sadhana of renunciation. If we reached this stage in our spiritual evolution, we have understood we are not the body, not the conditioned influences and not even the mind and its sense of an individual Soul /Spirit.

The Air Element asks us to let go of our small self altogether; there isn't even a unit made up of 'body, mind, spirit' but only pure life-force; pure existence, the great 'I **am'.**
It says in the Yoga Vashista:

The imagery world recedes from view
And falls like withered leaf
The intellect, cleared of the cloud of illusion,
Which veiled the deluded mind,
Shines as clear, as the vault of the autumn sky.

Ultimately 'Air' brings clarity and wisdom and the Sadhana is to cultivate concentrated, sharpened Discrimination…: not this, not that…..the highest teachings of this is called Vedanta…that which comes at the end, even of knowledge; the Vedas.

Worship now is focused on that which embodies the teachings, i.e. the teacher, the inner Guru - even the Teaching itself. But then what is that? One of the Wise of India, explained, what that means: 'I have', so he says '24 gurus, amongst them: Earth Water, Fire, Air and Space, the sun, the moon, a child, a spider, a dove and a tree etc. etc.'

We learn from everything around, once we open our vision and wisdom is accepted as knowledge and love to be found everywhere and in everything….. this means the Teacher, the teaching and the taught become one.

This changes the nature of worship; as the worshipped and the worshipper are not anymore Two-but One.

Now let's turn to the Space-Element, and its Sadhana.
As we mentioned above, here address elemental Space. Mother Space (Vrajavahari, in Tibetan Buddhism) holds all Creation in her lap; moreover she loves all her children equally.

The lesson we learn from Space is to be aware that all phenomena simply exists, as a result of **practicing this detachment**, we are no more bound to the perception about things of this world with likes and dislikes , desires and aversion. Sad things happen joy happens. It is, as it is. All the poles of opposites disappear from the mind; there is neither female nor male, neither past nor future. Physical manifestation just is, but is not important. A person like that, goes about the daily business, unperturbed; there is no more suffering (which is the result of our attachment). And yet the longing, the drive that has carried us to this point still exists.

The ever upward force, we call Udana Prana is still there, for ever urging to go deeper into contemplation and meditation. It pushes us to the frontier of meditation. It asks us what was it all for…this long journey of spiritual evolution we have been on. **What was /is the purpose of it all?** We evolved and practiced probably for many life-times… what was the purpose? And then we realize that at the very start we asked: Who am I?

Now we ask the same, but on a subtler level? *Who are we when we are our true selves?*

Gradually we grow, over long periods of journeying on the spiritual path to acknowledging that we *are that One about which we can say nothing.* And yet we struggle: Potential …. Intelligent energy…..Consciousness… Pure existence….Nothingness? The Yogic teachings say… **there is no explanation, no description of THAT............**But by practicing/ using a mantra in meditation, it will be revealed, known...beyond words…as pure experience…if you like. So we practice:
So Ham… I am That!

We have played and practiced surrender at various points…but always there was someone to surrender! Now the gap is closing… no **individual entity is left to surrender, t**he door has opened to Grace only! We finally understand, it's not the roles we play in life, nor how we are made up, nor the intellectual concepts we develop

of who we are......all this has gone...as so much 'lost words in Space'. What remains? Divine experience: I am That!
The journey is completed. All our effort now ceases. There is only Grace.

So what is the level and practice to be reached with the Space Element? **'Allowing' divine experience to happen.**

As long as there is someone, who can and wants to experience the divine ....it is only a phenomena happening in Elemental Space. Going beyond that, is ---- going beyond relative Space into absolute Space. The quality and sense attributed to relative Space is sound. To go beyond relative Space is entering Silence!

The final Sadhana of Space is Silence

PART I

Contemplation on Earth

Some places on this globe speak to us more than others; Cornwall is one such place that speaks to me, it makes me especially aware of the earth; ancient Celtic lore is intrinsically connected to the earth as the Mother Goddess, in fact, the valley I lived in is referred to as her landscape temple. In this place I am acutely aware of Earth!

But really every civilization generated their own myths and stories about this stable, seemingly immovable ground that with the 'kiss of rain' turns into a fertile field, abundantly supporting life. When we talk about the earth, we mean the planet, including all that is unfolding from it – when we talk of Earth, as one of the Five Elements, we mean simply 'the ground' …or do we?

Yes, the earth is the ground on which we stand; it locates us in space. Odd how we have no difficulty in accepting that plants and trees need to be firmly rooted in the ground or the wind will kill them; yet we forget that we too need to acknowledge our need for grounding. Of course we have a choice (in more ways than one) where and how. And each location on the 'body of earth' has different features and textures. In places earth has a loose surface of gravel and sand from where a weed is easily pulled up; in vast other areas that ground is covered by water; in yet other places she appears as the most waterlogged swamp where only specially adapted life can exist. In some, she has heavy clay soil, rich in minerals holding things firmly in their place and other places have wonderful, rich fertile soil where much can grow (and so on).

Nearly everywhere we find people, tribes and nations that have their roots firmly planted in the fields, paddies or forest, and not only people but also all manner of plants and animals. *Earth provides for all, there is no other source other than her.* And once we have lived, earth takes us back! All - good and bad, beautiful and ugly, she does not judge; **Earth holds all.**

As I hold a bit of earth in my hand and muse over its magnificence, I suddenly realize that not am I holding earth, but that the earth is actually holding me. The spot where my feet touch the ground, the earth is holding me; that I hold earth in the palm of my hand, is just another convenient illusion. Gravity, the core of earth, is holding both, so that we don't "fly off" or dissolve. It holds me, as I hold it. I could not hold it without being held by it. It gives total stability, unshakeable security to me and all else. She holds the trees, the houses, the water, the cars, the factories, the good people, the bad people, the crops and the weeds, the tiger and the mosquito. She holds all creatures whether we deem them useful or not, whether we deem them dangerous and harmful or not. She just holds!

What she holds goes through a cycle of change; seeds become plants, become trees, become rotten wood, become compost; becoming flowers, becoming seeds, to becoming plants; a baby lives, becomes an adult, grows old, dies - but at no time does the earth let go! There is no escaping; her job of holding is never done!

She is the playing field where Water, Fire and Air sport; throughout she remains stable, true to her task, holding without judging anything unworthy.

Not so long ago I sat in a Cornish Fogou to meditate. A Fogou is a prehistoric earth passage with one or two chambers; built into and fortified by granite boulders. It was reputedly used for ceremonies, healing or simply as a shelter in times of tribal fighting. To sit in the bowels of the earth reveals her potentiality. There is nothing but stillness, yet that stillness has almost tangible potency, a fullness that can only be experienced, not described. As womb she is also grave; beginning and end, life and death, death and rebirth – **life itself is contained in her**.

Hold a handful of Earth, smell it, see it, pinch it between your fingers; what is it that you actually hold? A mélange of many things! On a physical level we could answer: it is fibres, water, grains of sand, minerals, even crystals; a conglomerate also found on other planets! Then there is the chemical answer that talks about feldspars, lime, H_20, alkaline and acid balance, but also about pollutants, poisons, pesticides and radioactive waste.Then there is a biological answer; it talks about millions of microbes, living organisms, cells, plasma, plant fibre and more; compost really – embodying decay and fertility, the spectrum of Life.

Even the most barren looking desert sand holds microbes and seeds. It became abundantly clear to me when one day travelling through the centre of Australia, I witnessed a 'miracle.' It rained, and within a few hours the 'barren' desert-earth changed into fields of flowers as far as the eye could reach; a synergetic mixture where the whole has become stronger than all its parts. This mixture takes on a new character. **What is it then that we mean when talking of 'Earth'?**

My handful of earth used to be a granite boulder eroded during thousands of years, yet as much as it contains ancient particles, it contains last year's leaves and living organisms born today. 'Now!' Earth speaks of a stability that adapts - is not static; for earth a thousand years are no different than yesterday or tomorrow; **despite continuous change it maintains its integrity!**

Looking again at the handful of earth, I am reminded of my grandmother; on her sideboard she had a white china pot filled with earth. We used to lift the lid as children and look at its dark, almost black, crumbly consistency, and wondered how one could have 'dirt' as an ornament. But of course for her it was not an ornament, neither was it dirt, but a reminder of her homeland. She was a refuge from Silesia, and this handful of earth was her link to her past, and moreover it was her emotional support now. It was a link to her mother, and her mother's mother.

As we saw in the onset, many cultures consider 'earth' as mother. In Sanskrit (root of many of our familiar languages), the word for mother, for earth and for clay is the same: MATA. In Egypt, the syllable MA not only stood for mother but also meant to see, and the hieroglyph was that of an eye, its meaning was truth. **Earth, mother and truth** - powerful shared roots. The 'womb of all life' makes a strong image, no wonder she is heralded as the archetypal goddess, Gaia or Bhumi - a living organism, symbolizing truth and sacredness.

One night in a certain place in India, I went to bed, just as usual. As soon as I relaxed, my feet felt like they were on fire. The burning sensation turned to intense heat *inside* the soles of my feet; then I saw actual flames around my feet. It was so real, I was perplexed and disorientated, yet the fire crept up my legs, encircling my calves and stayed there with painful, consuming heat. Gradually the fire moved up to my hips and into my pelvis; there it stayed, for what seemed a long time - then moved up to my chest. My feet were engulfed in flames; the rest of me seemed burnt by that heat. I saw the flames, yet was not scared, more mesmerized as my thoughts repeated:

'I walked on sacred Earth; all day I walked barefoot on sacred Earth; walked on sacred Earth; stood on sacred ground.'

This awareness of earth as sacred was lost in our Western civilization due to the influence of a branch of Greek philosophy, which focused on 'soul-less-matter'. Such matter could be dissected, exploited, misused and destroyed at will, which is exactly where the focus on the material world took us.

However with the new physics, awareness returns to matter as intelligent light which communicates with the observer (and so earth becomes Earth again). Earth is not as our senses perceive - dense dead matter - but moving, conscious energy, even light. The Celts (and many indigenous people) were aware of this, and thus saw the world as both worldly and 'otherworldly', experiencing Earth as a divine (beyond human).

Travelling through the Rift Valley in Africa, this quality drew me to walk barefoot, sit, lie, meditate and gaze at Her; getting absorbed – lost to powerful feelings of a timelessness sense of mother qualities, of the origin of creation. Earth wisdom is knowing that we exist only within her. She holds us, she provides – into her we dissolve.

Earth itself teaches us to look deep into the centre of things, deep into the essence of ourselves. It teaches us to look beyond the appearance and discover our original nature as sacred beings. What looks like a handful of dust, or dirt, smells of compost (a musty, wet rotting material), tastes slightly sour and feels a mixture of rough particles and smooth slimy clay - is actually a form of divine consciousness, a form of light, a form of God.

Holding my handful of Earth – it fills me with awe! Matter shares consciousness; consciousness is awareness: as such earth is a living, intelligent organism that knows. There is only conscious energy, source and manifestation, sacred is profane and profane is sacred.

The Australia Aboriginals of the Northwest, especially in the Kimberleys, have a beautiful way to express this in the story of Nangina. He is the first man. Originally sleeping in the ground, he wakes up and discovers nature and all that is around him. He feels the power of the spirit in himself and he recognizes it as the source of all life. Although it is overpowering and he sees its frightening omnipotence, he bends it to his own will, using the energy of fire to transform his food, himself and his environment. Laying fire around his abode, he keeps his mountain of origin sacred, Ngalenga. In the act of naming things, he identifies himself with all things and their destiny, grass, birds and animals that have emerged from the earth. His own inner spirit gives them life by giving them names. As a 'spirit-being' he is a Wandjina; as an 'earth-being' he is Nangina, who takes a wife, gives her home and shelter, gives order and law and dreams a spirit-child into his wife's womb. Other tribesmen infringe on him and he imparts his wisdom to them, assuring continuity. Then he allows himself to be killed, to become a dream-painting on the walls of his place of origin; in this way his spirit merges back into the earth and becomes Wandjina, the sacred dream-time painting drawn with earth, on earth (rock). Nangina Wandjina the first man shows us: There is only One; Wandjina the original source is Nangina in its earthly form

Being in union with its different forms Earth instructs us to accept this world as it is! Be content.

Can we learn to be without judgment? It is hard; we judge people for wearing different clothes, having different hair or lifestyles or even for eating different food. We judge people because they laugh differently... talk differently... smile differently... play different games in the playground... buy different brands of consumer goods etc. Our judgment means we do not respect that person; worse even we deny them the sacred kinship.

We are in desperate need of re-educating our minds!

Not just for other people's sake, but for our own; we pass the most terrible judgments against ourselves: I am not good enough... capable enough... clever enough... slim enough; I am too big... too small... too timid... too loud... too ugly... too... These self-judgments are constantly reinforced by families, schools and society. Which parent has not fallen into the trap of calling their child too slow, too thin, stupid, fat etc.? Or less obvious: we call our children...

very clever... very beautiful... very talented etc. These judgments, positive or negative are harmful, and yet they are ingrained in our society; we take them as 'natural.' The only way out is… to stay in our Centre. To be like the Earth, firm in our acceptance of life as it is – **without judgment yet with compassion!**

The scriptures advocate a way out: awareness and discrimination. We need to open our ears, listen, understand and decide: that is not worth listening to! No need to judge. We need to open our eyes, see, understand and decide: that is not worth seeing!

No need to judge.

Usually, we are closed off, stuck in routines, and thus repeat the same old patterns of behaviour, of mistakes, of pains and disease. It is our lack of awareness and our profusion of judgments, which keeps us in quicksand, rather than fertile Earth.

Our judgments take ridiculous forms; we judge it as more profitable to live in an urban environment - but then feel isolated from nature, separate from life and lonely. We judge that eating a Hamburger is more important than the rain forest! (Cutting down forests to create grazing land for cattle). We judge that mining uranium for atomic power is more important than the sacred sites of the Australian Aboriginals; and commit genocide to an ancient culture.

By implication, I judge that burning petrol to drive my car is more important than the acid rains caused by exhaust fumes that destroy the forests. We judge that the street children of Brazil have less right to live than us, or we would not allow their poverty to drive them into the sewers. The list is endless. Our attitudes, built on *hidden judgments*, penetrate every niche and corner of our existence.

Let us wake up, and **learn from the Earth to hold creation safe, and be responsible without judgment, to hold and respect each other so we all can flourish**. Let us return from our musing thoughts to focus on the 'real earth.'

Have a look out of your window, or imagine being in a park. Look closely at the earth. On it lies a stone, it just lies there... see the tree, follow its root - they just root there, held by earth... See the person walking, the feet touch the ground, they just touch, held for just the right time by the earth. Earth holds the tree adequate to the tree's need, so that it will not get 'blown over.' Look at the house. It stands there; the earth provides it with a base. People walk, sit, run, even lie on the earth; it just holds them in whatever position they choose.

To appreciate earth, we would need to change our 'glasses.' Normally we look at a stone and think 'it is too grey,' it 'is useless,' etc. We look at the tree thinking, 'it needs pruning;' ' it is big; too big?' or we might even think: ' it is beautiful;' yet all this - positive or negative - is built on judgments.

We never see the earth reject something because it is ugly, or hold something too tight because it is beautiful; can you see how holder and held co-operate? We look at the house and say: "How cosy it nestles in the valley," or "how dangerous it is so close to the road." We look at the people and think: 'He is careless walking on the grass.' We look and our mind judges; we see the world around us through a veil of conditioned judgment; the sad thing is that we miss appreciating what we really see. If we really look, without our judgmental projections, we see earth's **self-less generosity.**

We too can give such self-less service to our children, our parents, our community, our employers, our friends and our enemies. A mother provides selfless service, without knowing whether her love will ever be returned by baby, child or adult. She holds and loves without expectation of reward! Yet if the mother does not take care of herself with adequate rest, food, enjoyment and so on, she will not be able to provide for the baby. Self-less does mean 'without ego' – not 'without caring for oneself!'

In the Mahabharata, one of India's most revered texts is a section where Krishna explains that the duty of a warrior is to fight 'with detachment from the fruit of his labours.' This is selfless- service; to do what is necessary with detachment from 'the fruits of our labours' is most foreign to us. We cannot imagine to - 'just give,' 'just do' - without thinking of the result, because we want to achieve something, get somewhere. We want the fruits, and to eat them. And we forget that as soon as we have eaten them, hunger and desire raises again the desire to yet get another fruit to eat. The 'desire' to have, never seems to sleep.

How self-less, generous action can be performed, we need to learn from the earth. We need to re-educate the mind, cultivate a different attitude: something in our mind-make-up has to shift.
To give quality time to our children, rather than dash off "doing our own thing"- that is not easy.
To do a job well (even cleaning the toilet) without expecting to be praised or paid, is not so easy.
To give a friend, partner, husband or wife love, acceptance and support, without waiting for them to love us in return; that is not

so easy.
To give to the poor, sick and old of our time, care and love without thinking: I hope one day in heaven (or in my own old age) this good deed will be rewarded; this is very difficult for us.

We are brought up in a culture where the thought prevails: if we simply **give generously, without wanting something in return** 'we would never get anywhere!' To give freely is difficult, because we judge the giver, judge the gift, and judge the act. "Aunt Sue was 'unfair' to give me some socks for Christmas! She should have thought more 'what I want'; I don't like the socks." This is not the way of the Earth - she is **infinitely patient with us**.

Driving around this weekend, I am reminded of the patience of the earth. She does not rebel when we pour hot tarmac all over her; when we bore holes into her, spray her with pesticides and even bury toxic chemicals or radioactive waste in her. She holds it all, processing it with infinite patience, transforming it to the good of all, even if it needs thousands of years (as in the case of nuclear waste). Such patience is timeless; we need to learn from the earth!

I m p o s s i b l e, you might say! "No business can survive on that, we need to innovate, change, grow, act, push, press! There is no growth without push. Not even learning can be without the desire to acquire knowledge! If we are content and sit on our backside, nothing progresses - no science, health or educational program can be carried out if we are content with the status quo."

W r o n g! **Contentment** doesn't mean doing nothing- it means doing the appropriate thing! How can we recognise right, appropriate action? By forgetting what we want the outcome to be; simply doing what is necessary.

There is, no doubt, a lot more to contemplate about the Earth; I leave you to proceed on you own journey of contemplating the richness of the earth's teachings. But before that, let us summaries: Earth is that energy-field, that form of energy, which holds the potential for physical evolution; it is rich and plentiful. It shares its riches generously; it nurtures and supports indiscriminately; it is non-judgmental, giving. It synthesizes opposites (life and death); it stabilizes, balances. Earth is the quiet centre around which activity revolves; it is tireless in serving others; it preserves (family, society), it is compassionate and sympathetic to all in need, it re-cycles; it is strong, it holds and protects.

It is these attributes that are the treasure of what we call Earth; it is these attributes that we can learn from Her, who we call Earth.

Contemplation on Water

In front of me on the desk, is a glass of water; in it the water is clear, I can see through it, it is crystal clear, has no colour of its own. Water fills the glass, takes on its shape without effort. If I spill it, it adapts to the shape of the floor. In fact water adapts to any shape, be it a glass, syringe, bathtub, sewage pipe, river or ocean. It takes up the form of *that which limits it.* It is so **adaptable** that it appears as though it constantly gives up its integrity - although it never does.

When the raindrop gives up its existence to become the pool, it remains 'water'; when the dewdrop gives up its existence and becomes the sap of a tree - it still remains 'water.' Or less romantic: when the water in a steam-engine evaporates – it remains water. Furthermore it always seeks to merge with the bigger version of what it is already. However long the journey water is – one drop merges with another, one river merges with another and ultimately the river becomes the ocean, *giving up its separate identity.* This drive to merge with something greater seems to be the secret and reason why the confluences of rivers are held sacred in Indian and other cultures. This aspect of water has inspired many great thinkers and philosophers to use water as a symbol *for all that we are, yet need to become;* i.e. Ultimate Reality. The Chinese idea of the Tao as the watercourse way, is merely one such example.

There is a story told about one of the great Christian Sages:
St. Augustine went to the great ocean; he watched some boys playing with cups. He walked over to them and asked them: 'What are you doing?' The boys tried to explain that with their cups, they were trying to empty the ocean. They filled the cup, walked it to the

beach and emptied the water onto the sand. They continued their feverish, but fruitless attempt with great diligence. St. Augustine with his rational scholarly attitude said: 'can you not see that your vessels can't contain the vastness of the ocean; you will never succeed in scooping the ocean out, you will have to find a different way!'

The boys looked at each other, smiled - and threw their cups into the ocean. Running away happy. The childish prank revealed to St. Augustine, that only by complete abandonment, can one lose oneself in the Absolute. Only through the awareness of being part of it, can we 'fathom the ocean'.

In accordance with many wisdom teachings, we can contemplate our individual lives as waves dancing on the ocean; or indeed as whirlpools in the river of consciousness. Concentrated life-energy dances for a while – as 'me' in this dimension of reality we call earth

- then continues with the flow of the river of life, - finally pouring itself into the ocean. All the while 'water is playing,' essentially nothing has changed; snowflake/wave/whirlpool **surrender** their individual temporary form - and yet remain 'water'.

But let's come back to the glass of water in front of me! What happens if I drink this water? It becomes part of me; it fills my veins and cells; I become the container – all be it not a 'watertight one.' My skin is porous (sweating); my lungs absorb and give out moisture. There is humidity /water outside me…and inside me… how much water is only a question of degree. We cannot survive in an atmosphere devoid of Water. In fact, with a bit of humour we can see that we live in 'water' not much different from fish! At present I am temporarily in Singapore and the humidity is so high, that this idea does not seem that far from the truth.

However high the humidity outside me, there is more water (78 %) inside me, although in various disguises: as tissue fluid, blood, lymph, spinal fluid etc. In fact I need to drink this water in order to maintain these fluid levels, in order to stay healthy or even alive. But unlike the water in the glass in front of me, the water in me is not pure.

Water not only adapts in shape but also to the needs of the host, i.e. it accommodates or rather - carries loads of 'foreign matter', such as chemical substances i.e. iron, nutrients, minerals etc. Once water is engaged in the job of carrying these - which seemingly dissolve in water, we call it: blood, lymph or bile. Water fulfils this job as a carrier of other substances in many circumstances; it carries medicines with as much equanimity as poison, viruses, pollution, acid, even atomic waste, without regrets, without effects on its true nature. Water is **receptive** to the extreme. This detached receptivity gives it incredible power. As seawater it contains all other elements and thus it has the power of all of them (which is another indication of why many spiritual traditions use it as a potent symbol). Water contains the warmth of fire (without it, it would be ice). It also contains some oxygen (air), salts of the earth and, it occupies space. How then does it maintain its integrity?

Its flexibility, its adaptability makes it possible for water to regenerate. For example: after the water has been through my body nurturing me by carrying the nutrients through me thus fulfilling one function, it leaves me – carrying away unwanted chemicals – carrying out another function. Its *flexibility allows it to change purpose (adapts).* After the water leaves me (finally) it will end up entering the ground; in earth it lets go of the collected poisonous (negative) substances; it deposits them on sand grains, cleaning itself! This process of **filtering things out** is a mutual service between earth and water. Water contributes its ability to dissolve anything (good, bad - useful or not - who is the judge)? Then earth accepts the additives which water has transported, and reconstitutes them.

This cleansing process takes Water into great depth from where it cleanses and rejuvenates itself. Once water has seeped deep into the bowels of the earth, through layers and layers it rests at the deepest point and from there it re-emerges as a spring. Thus having cleaned itself, it is available again to serve.

This process is referred to on metaphysical level in the Maitreya Upanishad (115):

'Washing with the soil of knowledge and the water of detachment is called true purification. It is the purification which brings purity to the mind and destroys the three tendencies (mental habits).'

In the physical dimension Earth and Water co-operate in this action of cleansing, of regeneration, in fact they are mutually dependent in this. If we harm the earth, we harm the water and vice versa!

Water pulled by Earth's gravity sinks deep, but gravity also acts on water in a different context: That very same force resides in the moon, the pull of gravity from there is responsible for the tidal movement of oceans. This pull of gravity on Water can be felt also in man and woman. This is frequently experienced as physical 'tidal waves', which can be felt in the sacro-spinal fluid or 'emotional tidal waves' (mood-swings).

Mans psyche or emotional expressions are likened to Water. Just as Water is pulled in the depths of the earth - where cleansing and rejuvenating takes place, at times the human being sinks into the depth of doubt and existential fear, this is referred to as 'the dark night of existence', or 'nausea of existentialism' and is the despondency described by such authors as Camus and Sartre.

That state might be experienced as fear and depression – as a 'dark mood' with 'absence of light' however it harbours the chance to cleanse and rejuvenate and rise to higher awareness.

The metaphor used by Christian Mystics such as St. Anthony (Egypt, 251-356 AD) is the 'dark night of the soul'. His biographer writes about his life in the barren desert, 'He cried, wrestling himself from his seat, he leapt up as if to run from the cave, when he gasped - because there they were before him, the dark and twisted forms of demons. Were they women or men or animals? Were they creatures from some unspeakable nether region? He could not tell...' Only later St. Anthony understood 'let us not contemplate horrors in the soul nor invent fears for ourselves... let's take courage and always rejoice... the enemies' actions correspond to the condition in which they find us; they pattern their phantoms after our own thoughts.'

How much more 'Yogic" could be his insight, to see that the patterns and images of our fears are made by our mind, and as the Yoga Sutras remind us, we need to replace those negative trends with positive, joyful images or vibrations. For that we have to become Masters of our minds. Resting in the depth, in deepest, stillest part of the ocean where nothing moves, there is clarity, there is a potent stillness. There is silence. It is such silence which we try to experience in meditation, where the mind has left the surface waves and rests in its own being. From the depth of the stillness, from the process of **self-cleansing**, of purification water resurfaces as pure 'spring-water'.

The process of water sinking into the depth of the bowels of the earth has another ‘side ‘to it, we have touched on previously. Once water has found the level of ground water, there it gathers in underground pools, *merging with the company of the like and together they rise!*

We said at the beginning, water takes up the form of ‘what limits it’. An individual is a very limited being! It is limited by its own conditioning, once this limiting pollution has been deposited, given up left behind in the dark depth…, water joins other pure waters together and surfaces as gushing springs. One could say water is so flexible it adapts and merges to other forms of itself.

Pure clean spring-water (water of life) emerges to form a brook and from there begins its cyclic journey of nurturing. Water fulfils its dharma of nurturing life; the brook nurtures the mosses and flowers! Soon though, it changes shape again; evaporating through the leaves of the plant as it joins the mist of the early summer day; after dancing in the morning air it falls back into the stream. The stream gets visited by animals, they drink; thus water becomes bird, elephant and mouse. The stream receives water back from the animals and flows on, becoming a river, possibly via the electricity factory, where it becomes part of big turbines. But however many cycles there are to its life, eventually the river pours itself into the ocean – but water’s journey is not finished! It merely starts another cycle. Evaporating, it forms the clouds, which drop as rain, being absorbed in the earth, sinking deep into its bowls until emerging again….

We can see the parallel in the life of the Boddhisattva or Saint. Spending his life in tireless service nurturing, purifying others and even when the cycle of life seems finished, *That One*, returns to continue in another **cycle of egoless service.**

Inherent in the Water-energy is this quality of adaptability that at best continuously nourishes others. Hence we recognize the dharma; the such-ness of water is **to nurture**. It is used by others and then returns to reconstitute itself - only to serve again. No surprise that water is called 'life-sustaining,' 'life-giving' even 'water of life'; due to this quality it is also known **as symbol of female energy**, especially in the context of healing.

Looking at the ancient Hebrew (writing used no vowels- nkvh/ nkbh) the word for the feminine is 'nekevah,' and waterhole 'nikbah,' the words are almost identical!

The Bulgarian born, French spiritual master Omraam Mikhael Aivanhov, (1900-1986) writes: 'Water is the mother of Life and we owe it gratitude and respect.... Water is sustaining, nourishing... water is love...let the water flow… water starts with love...' loving service.

Celtic wells (still used in contemporary Britain, esp. Cornwall and Ireland) have since time immemorial been connected to female goddesses; early on in our Era this tradition has merged with Christian Saints, for their connection to female healing energy (fertility). Wherever water gushed forth, Anu the great mother of gods is venerated, in whatever guise and preserved in the name, i.e. Bride-well; St. Anne's Well; Brighid or St. Brigid's Well; St Buryana's Well etc. etc.

In Greek and Roman history Nymphs and healing springs were common. In the Cult of Asclepius (the great healer) water is considered as sacred and associated with goddesses, nymphs or even a god. Even today in rural Greece, people will refuse to take their midday rest by a spring for fear of 'Nereids' or nymphs who might get you 'with child.'

In Australian Aboriginal myth, female Goddesses or maidens guard the water-hole; they bring and harbour fertility; Ankotarinja, original man, first recognizes his personal self- by looking into water and later needs to go to the waterhole to discover female beauty and 'wetness', in order to become 'the other.'

In India great rivers are female; one speaks of the Mother Ganga (Ganga Mai,) and equally of the Narmada River. It is said that Shiva was in such strenuous ascetic trance, that rivulets of sweat flowed from him and took on the form of a woman; one moment she was a beautiful virgin, the next a dancing girl and even a seductress. This play of female energy amused Shiva so much that he named HER Narmada (Delightful One), blessing her with the words: 'You shall be forever holy, forever inexhaustible.' Then he gave her to the most illustrious of all suitors, the Ocean, Lord of all rivers; she flowed, delightfully sparkling, into her lover's arms.

Another of 'Shiva's locks' is Saraswati; once a mighty river, with a tremendous culture on its banks, which sunk at the end of the last ice-age below the Himalayan sands. Yet still today a powerful gurgling stream remains in the Western Himalayas. SHE, Saraswati is revered as the eternal stream of knowledge and wisdom. When I visited the little shrine by the waterfall where she breaks with tremendous power from between the rocks – the shrine was decorated with fresh flowers, honoured by Her people.

Why might **wisdom be associated with Water?**
Since ancient times, in many cultures we come across this idea that Water has memory!

In today's world Homeopathic medicine is probably the best known version. (Medicines diluted to such an extent, that no original molecule of the 'ingredient' remains –however 'Water retains its memory and heals with it.' Another well-known testimony to this are the Flower Remedies of Edward Bach (1934), who wrote, 'The action of these remedies is to raise our vibrations and open up our channels for the reception of the Spiritual Self, to flood our natures with the particular virtue we need, and wash out from us the fault that is causing the harm.'

In 1988 the French scientist Ben Benvenista (and later Prof. M. Ennis) proved that water takes up the knowledge of the medicine. But in our days, the Japanese Professor Emoto with his photography of water crystals in various circumstances probably had the most spectacular impact. He showed beyond doubt that water retains knowledge/vibrations, be they positive or negative ones.

The ancients were right - water has memory! This quality of water to retain subtle knowledge is used in many ways.

Some mix salt into it for purification rites, light candles or burn incense while reciting formulas or mantras over water, claiming that water retains the 'spirit of it and should be greeted with great love and respect. Others ask the 'Angel of water' for blessing before it is drunk. This might seem 'way out,' but people like Gigi Capriolo (Cosmos Centre in Milan) support this; he assures that the waters of the Ganges, the Jordan and the well at Lourdes have the special holy vibration, especially for this very reason. The more people pray at a holy shrine/well the more the water takes up these vibrations. It remembers!

Have you ever stood at sunset or sun-rise by the sea, or at a lake... and observed how the light of the sun is reflected by water? Water, still water reflects the light, the light of wisdom. Many Buddhists path refer to this, water's quality of reflecting the light of wisdom.

But, you might intervene - water is not only peaceful, soft, gentle, receptive and nurturing and beautiful with its reflection of light. Water has also great strength and at times turns it into violence; how about excessive monsoon rains, killer floods, terrible freak waves, as the tsunamis etc. Water can carry the greatest boulders downstream! Sea levels rise and drown whole islands and continents, rivers cut enormous canyons to follow their course with unbending will and drive to get to the ocean. Rain wears down the highest mountain.

Yes and because of these aspects, water is associated with **willpower and the strength of discipline**. Here is the root of the metaphorical saying that drops of the softest water will in time wear down even the hardest stone.

Water just does not give up! Why? Its **drive to fulfil its dharma** is unerring: it has to get to the next level in order to take the water to the sea, come what may! And if something is in the way, water works at it until it gets through. Water, one could say, has great **determination**.

Determination and adaptability have led to many myths about **shape-shifting.** It is referring to the ability to not only rejuvenate, but reinvent oneself. In shamanic traditions a human is considered able to retain intelligence and memory - yet take on animal forms to attain a certain purpose, to fulfil a certain dharma, to defeat a certain situation, or attain a certain quality. Man becomes beast, frog becomes prince, Lords turn into stags, wizards turn into eagles etc. In Celtic lore, the Irish hero Tuan (St. Finnian of Morvilla) becomes a stag, a wild boar, a hawk and a salmon until he is born with full memory of all his previous existences - making the point that one lives in order to gather knowledge.

King Arthur is taught by Merlin to be a badger and a hawk, in order to learn tenacity and patience. Mongan, in the Book of Fermoy, takes up shapes of animals in water, land and air in order to learn the qualities of each element.

The famous ballet 'Swan Lake,' is based on the Celtic legend of Aengus mac Os, the god of love and youth who falls into profound lovesickness, until he discovers that his love is Caer Iborneith, who spends most of her time in the shape of a swan. Through magic music he learns to take her shape in order to woo her.

The Celtic word for 'shape-shifting' is tuirgin: a fluid transition from one form into another (Cormac's Glossary). In a deep state of meditation we experience such transition into 'the fourth dimension,' a reality beyond the ordinary perception - the word for this state in Sanskrit is *turiya*, the words are uncannily similar.

We can learn from this ability of water to transcend, it enables us to feel into other people, to 'shift our awareness into another'; it teaches us to suspend our own personality, its wants and wishes – But that takes courage, training and determination. I heard a lovely little story about a small stream. It flows happily along, then it comes to a stretch of desert:

‘I am so afraid, if I get on with my journey, I will be absorbed by the sand.’ So the sands whisper, ‘Don’t worry, just change yourself and jump into the arms of the wind.’ But the fear has a tight grip on the little river; as its worry of absorption by the sand increases, it takes courage and jumps into the air, changing its shape into vapour. The wind comes and picks it up and carries it gently across the desert; at the end of the desert, at a mountain top, the wind carefully puts down the water and as it rains down, the stream resumes its course.

The stream needed to overcome its fear of losing itself, and then it could shift its shape: and this is the key for continuing life’s purpose. It could not have done it if it had clung to its limiting form, its conditioned self, its personality. Like the stream, we have to put aside the previous limiting patterns, forms and shapes so that via the experience of nothingness, of pure emptiness (or pure clear water) and self-purification, we can continue service unclouded by our own personality.

This clarity is freedom, is being free from all colour, all movement, all past and present, **this crystalline clarity of still water** – is a stillness/emptiness filled with potential. Being ‘without shape’ gives the freedom to take any shape.

This is a marked difference to the nurturing generosity of earth giving space and time to the other - **water becomes the other!**

On a physical level, water becomes food, on the psychological and spiritual level, it becomes the teaching.

All very well, you might say, but we live in a highly industrialized society, with high crime-rates, disrupted families, pollution, overpopulation, aggressive kids, competitive and exploiting business and more. How can **being adaptable, nurturing and flexible** help us in our high tech, daily lives?

Here is another story: An aggressive eleven-year old school child has frequently been reprimanded for disruptive class behaviour, but to no avail. He has even been noted for bullying. His work too, leaves much to be desired. He is threatened with having to leave school. When the parents are called in for consultation, they seem not to mind his low marks, they consider him 'stupid anyway, as long as he does his best, it's OK with us.' They also describe aggressive behaviour at home.

Imagine one of the teachers has the above qualities of 'Water'. She observes that in Karl's artwork he uses bold brushwork and dark colours, he does not like details. In English lessons, she notices that his reading, writing and spelling are way below average. She also notices that he gets aggravated when observed; he cannot cope with attention.

The first thing the teacher does is to give him space; she gives him little jobs to do where he can be alone, such as looking something up in the dictionary; mixing some special paints etc. Sometimes she joins him, so they can be 'private.' This way he isn't exposed and feels secure enough to make remarks about his family, how the rooms are so crowded, that he never has time or space to do anything because his brothers and sisters are always doing something or having the TV on or...

Putting herself into such living conditions, the teacher senses that in order to have privacy, he shuts off, then, disturbed in his 'cocoon,' he becomes angry and aggressive, a 'hedgehog syndrome.' Having identified his problem, the teacher can then take measures to nourish him. She gives him bigger, solitary assignments and encourages other teachers to do the same. As the boy seems to enjoy that, he is offered the chance to do his homework in the office of the school secretary, where no one will bother him. His work becomes cleaner and better, and no more bullying is reported.

Obviously the school could do nothing to improve his home situation, but by giving him what he needed his behaviour and achievements improved. The teacher acted in the 'way of water:'!

Nature is Herself a book of wisdom from which to learn, if only we can open our hearts and minds to do so. Then we can learn from water's flexibility, learn to adapt and be receptive; we can learn how to filter out the unwanted, harmful stuff and thus purify ourselves. We can learn to feel into others, nurture them and serve, ego-less. We can learn from water how to grow in wisdom and how to use willpower and determination to fulfil our dharma. But most of all we can learn how to surrender without fear of losing our identity.

Contemplation of Fire

There is hardly a culture that has not a myth about fire and its source, the sun. For mankind, fire has always had two strong connotations: a great helper and a powerful destroyer. Its inherent power might have been the reason why Zeus wanted to keep fire out of reach of man. Yet Prometheus, with the intention of giving mankind protection from the elements, stole the fire from the Gods and gave it to humans. For this Zeus punished him severely, and sent a flood to earth to quench the uncontrollable fire.

Some main characteristics of fire are immediately clear: **it inspires, it protects, yet it is dangerous** and can become beyond our control.

I have a matchbox and a candle in front of me. I strike the match on the box and a flame comes with which to light the candle. Fire comes into existence by **friction** between two different components i.e. sticks, stones or matches – and/or massive collisions of energy/ matter in space. Let us, however, focus on the earthly version.

Through friction (release of inherent energy) a spark is created and exists in its own right, for a short time – but to grow and to last it has to be fed and nourished. However, its growth has to be monitored carefully, for further sparks easily fly off and create new fires. The growing spark itself increases rapidly in size and intensity, while its host is consumed equally rapidly. Combustible material while sacrificing itself, allows fire to grow while its own form is destroyed.

A candle flame looks harmless enough, yet what makes its flame, is the burning of wick and wax… both give up their present existence to become flame. Fire cannot be separated from its burning power – nothing to burn – no fire! Fire **destroys while it creates**. It transforms one thing, one form of matter into another. It transforms wood into ashes/chemicals…which then nourish next year's daffodils. In this way (on the base level) fire transforms matter into another form of matter. There is however a sinister aspect to this: watch a grass fire! Fire "eats" Grass! But watch what happens then… finished in one place, the fire proceeds, going on to take the next bits of grass! Behind it is devastation; fire can't go back over the same ground – there is nothing for it to feed on; there is no going back - no past, just death.

And moreover keep watching as the grass fire reaches a path! There might be more burn-able grass growing beyond the path, but when the fire reaches the path it dies for lack of burning material. **Fire has no past** - but also it has **no sense of future, it only exists right now.** It lives totally in the present. Contemplate it!

What it leaves behind are minerals, base chemicals that form more earth; mix that with water, only then future begins, but not the future of fire, by itself it has no future - it needs feeding by the "other" .

And that is not all. There are by-products of this process. Flames give off energy which we experience as heat or as kinetics; but the most noted by-product of this transformation (the wick of the candle being burned to ashes)…is light!

Yes, Fire is **the power of transformation,** we could say in Yoga speak: Fire is the Shakti of transformation. But She works on two distinct levels: the gross manifest (matter into matter, one form into another) and on transforming gross to subtle levels – matter turns to light! In ourselves, this transformation, this process of burning… is effort, is pain, is ***tapasya***; the very destruction of the old - makes way for new creation.

In the new creation fire is **joyous, glorious, happy** – hence we celebrate the new with Fire (the New Year; the new season, the new life (birthday) etc.) We use Fire for celebrating and honouring light….many cultures mark the equinoxes of the sun by lighting Fires.

Just to give one example: On the most south-western tip of UK (Cornwall) in a direct line-up, with the setting sun, on a hilltop, since long before the Christian Era bonfires are lit. From there, when the fire is seen on the next hill, the next fire is lit. In this way a beacon of light races throughout the island, honouring the longest day; celebrating the annual pinnacle of light.

When we talk about Fire as the material form of light we are in good company. Scientists tell us that light, might very well be the building block of the universe. In Yoga speak we talk of the Divine Light beyond all form. On the highest and subtlest level that Divine limits itself, gives up its subtle form to manifests in the perceptible universe, becoming a form that we can recognize with our senses. One form transforming into another, light manifesting in fire - fire dissolving in light; the power of transformation!

This power is never still. You might have seen Shiva dancing in a ring of Fire! Fire, the power that is never still, simultaneously destroying and creating.

There is much benefit in contemplating the various forms of fire: Contemplate the awesome power of wild, destructive forest fires, killing the green lungs of the planet – killing the producers of the very oxygen that it needs to burn. Think about a hungry straw fire that flares up brightly, yet dies almost immediately, having devoured its fuel.

Fire in its destructive form is awesome yet it is completely dependent on the immediate source of its existence, its food! If there is nothing more to burn it dies instantly! Burning-transformation is its "inherent nature", its dharma. As water's dharma is to flow and to nourish, Fire's dharma is to burn and transform. Fire, like each of the Elements manifests on a huge scale, it has – even seemingly opposite, characteristic (just like ice and vapour are both water). Contemplate the flame of a candle versus the inferno of a nuclear holocaust!

Out of the many aspects of fire, we will contemplate two aspects: **fire in the hearth** and the **sun, source of all fire.**

Let us first focus on the comforting glow of a fireplace or hearth; most of us will have enjoyed watching its gentle, dancing flames. Albert Einstein (theory of relativity) and Max Plank (quantum physics) both started their inquiries by observing apparent anomalies of light in front of an ordinary fireplace.

The process of burning uses and generates energy which is given off as warmth - **and light**. Light being a certain vibration of electromagnetic energy we receive and use to interpret our world. In the case of the fire of the fireplace it signals **safety, rest and security**. In Greek mythology, this slow burning fire is presided over by the Greek goddess Hestia. She is felt to be present in the living flame of the round fire that used to be in the centre of the home, temple and city. Her symbol was (just as in many cultures) a circle; she was worshipped not in an image or statue, but as a spiritually felt presence, embodied in the sacred fire, that provided illumination, warmth and heat. She was the oldest sister of the first generation of Olympian Gods, yet took no part in their affairs of love and war. Homer describes how Zeus gave her - instead of a wedding gift - the central place of the house, so that she could receive the best offerings.

Her Roman equivalent is Vesta; in her temples the sacred, central fire was tended by 'vestal virgins.' Her companion was Mercury, the messenger. He guarded the fire and the temple, representing the outgoing quality of the element Fire. The two belonged together yet they were not involved in each other; meaning fire does not have to go outward, **it can be contained, working inner most!**

Hestia stands for those that have controlled the wildness of fire and have learned to avoid being caught up in passion of the moment. Hestia is not attached to people, possessions, prestige or power. She feels whole, warm and content as she is. Her fire is the spiritual link to others; that literally would be carried as an ember from the temple to the houses and even from the house and taken on a journey.

These embers were symbolic of the steady glow of the divine fire in us. The Latin word for the hearth is 'focus,' *contained fire is focus*, is concentrating, is being totally absorbed, perceiving things by looking inward and intuitively sensing what is going on. This perception is shared in Chinese, Indian and many other traditions. In Yoga speak: **Intense focus, is Tapasya, the burning, purifying fire.** This relative tamed fire is very different from my second choice of contemplation.

I am sitting in front of a big 'French window'; the day is overcast yet somewhere out of my sight, is the sun. A huge ball of fire, or rather, of hot gas. Its outer periphery is still 6000 degrees Celsius hot; such heat is beyond our imagination. Its heat is the result of constant nuclear fusion. Yes, our beloved sun is a cauldron of constant nuclear **explosions.** The energy set free in these processes makes the sun 'shine.' Giant tongues of hot gas are whirled off the surface into space, much further than the atmosphere around the earth. Sometimes particles from these enormous explosions hit the earth and when they reach us they cause the beautiful lights we call aurora.

The vast temperatures we know of in the core of the earth are nothing compared to the temperatures reached in the stars and sun, where matter turns into gas and eventual dissolution into…! **And yet this unimaginable destructive power is the same one that**

gives us life. For us this awesome power is beneficial – because it's far away! We can't see or experience the activity of the fierce, boiling cauldron; we are safe because it is *exquisitely,* ***minutely balanced*** in distance. A cosmic law holds us just right; a bit closer we would melt, a bit further we would freeze! An amazing insight in the delicate balance, the careful control inherent in taming the fire! For fire to be beneficial it needs to be tamed, contained, or in Yogic terms turned inward.

In many traditions and esoteric literature, the sun is worshipped in recognition of its life-giving light, its **radiance; its splendour!** On an inter-religious conference I met a Shaman from the Shwar, indigenous people of the Amazon, who stated categorically that: there can be no life without Aruta, *Padre de LUZ,* - father of light. In the Judeo/Christian tradition the light is also frequently used to describe divine truth:

'While you have the light, trust the light,
The Lord is my light and my salvation.' (Ps. 27,1)
Christ said: 'I am the light of the world' (St. John 8,12)

Many traditions worship this radiant light as a God. In Egypt, Ra sailed across the skies; in ancient Persia, the Sun God rode in his chariot. In the northern Philippines Manaue, the Sun God lives in the treetops; for the Celts, the sun is a charioteer riding across the sky. Today in the South American Mountains, Indians still go into the mountains just like their forefathers, and worship the sunrise. During man's history some of the greatest constructions of mankind have been built to worship the sun, e.g. the Sun Pyramid in Mexico or Stonehenge in England, the Sun Temple at Konark, India. Furthermore, Kings derived authority for their lineage from the sun such as the Japanese Emperor (who is said to be a descendant of

Amataresu, the Sun), or Louis XIV (the French: Roi du Soleil, - King of the Sun), or descendants of the Raghuvansh royal line in ancient India, who claimed to have descended from the sun.
Even today, our 'sun- worshippers' fill the beaches all over the world!

The wise of India celebrated the sun as Surya, associated with life-creating energy and timely dissolution this was celebrated in Fire ceremonies, *Yajnas.* Surya guides us to righteousness and **inspires wisdom**; he is the eye of God, (as well as our eye), because through him, we can see the love of God and the love in each other. As such the inner 'sun,' the sun of love, is soul and points beyond the individual. Even today we say about someone we love, that the sun shines out of his/her eyes.

Swift and beautiful are you,
0 Sun, maker of the Light,
Who illumines all the radiant sky
Gazing beyond the dark we reach
The supreme Light and attain the Sun,
The God of gods, the Light. (Rig Veda, 1.504)

In Indian mysticism, the sun is still worshipped every morning by the offering of water poured unto the earth for brilliance of sight. The sun, due to whose light alone I can see, is itself an ordinary star - just as the other billions and billions which we see in the sky. To worship the sun as God, points beyond the physical to 'that which illumines out of itself.' The **Self-luminous** is absolute power behind everything. Out of this understanding the *Gayatri* is born, allegedly one of the oldest, most potent prayers in the world:

Tat Savitur varenyam: That most beautiful, brilliant light, the solar orb, that gives birth to all
Bhargo devasya dhimahi: May that Divine burning One, so fill my person that I become that light
Dhiyo yo nah pracodayãt: May being That, be my meditation.

***

There is another aspect worth contemplating about the sun. The sun's instant combustion throws off light and heat, generating conditions on earth, in which life can be generated, but in the process sun destroys itself in time (so the scientists tell us).

Remember what we said earlier about the candle... the wick and wax burn - give up their existence - to bring about the flame. No wonder at the origin of ancient wisdom is the idea of **sacrifice**! Every aspect of life on this earth is in one way or another fed by the gigantic fire – the giant sacrifice, the giant transforming power that is the sun. Even creatures that live in the dark, deep oceans can only exist there because the sun keeps the ocean from freezing.

Moreover a piece of plastic is not immediately recognized as 'sun-made'; yet even plastic containers are made from fossil oil (petrochemicals) which are compressed plant fibre (having stored solar energy) from long ago. Whatever we look at, sooner or later will be revealed as a form of sun energy. It brings us right back to modern science, where matter is light and light becomes matter – and that includes us.

Sacrifice always **serves and precedes new form** – it is ultimately positive, creative, life-giving. This life-affirming quality has been throughout the ages **associated with love; making everything positive and good.** Many mystics have seen and described it:

I am light itself, reflected in the heart of everyone;
I am the treasure of the Divine Name
The shining Essence of all things
I am every light that shines,
Every ray that illumines the world.
From the highest heavens to the bed-rock of the earth
All is but a shadow of my blazing Light.
If I dropped the veil covering my true essence
The world would be gone- lost in a brilliant light.

(Fakhruddin Araqui/Sufi,1213-1289)s

When talking about light, the boundaries between sunlight and God-light seem to disappear only too easily. How can we understand it? We know that all we normally perceive is vibrating energy yet we see it as different objects, forms and colours because sunlight is **reflected** or refracted much like a sunbeam in a glass of water. This 'reflected light' our mind interprets and labels according to our conditioning: green tree; red flower; brown hair etc. thus the world appears to us as millions of objects. Moreover, when our senses receive these vibrations and interpret them, this evokes feelings in us. These feelings we label according to certain frequency bands of light and as such their range is attributed to the Five Elements. What this seemingly absurd idea tells us is **that everything we see is in fact vibrating light,** light that originally comes from the sun.

It might seem strange to you but be assured, it is in accord with scientists, mystics and poets. The Element Fire **illumines** not just the 'objects' of the world, but our very thoughts, hearts and minds. Indeed the greatest human achievement is to be illuminated, to reach the state of *'En-lightenment,'* where we can see things for what they are… and not what label/concepts we project on them. In 'The Divine Comedy' Dante Alighirie writes:

> So dazzling was the splendour of that ray,
> that I must certainly have lost my senses …
> 0 light eternal fixed in itself alone...
> here my powers rest from their high fantasy,
> but already I could feel my being turned -
> instinct and intellect balanced equally
> as in a wheel whose motion nothing jars -
> by the love that moves the Sun and the others stars.

Dante's testimony bears witness to the power of such insights and the transformation that results.

Fire transforms darkness into light (this is the true meaning of the word *Guru*); equally it transforms light into matter: plants, trees, animals, people etc., and yes, it transforms clay into ceramics, ore into gold and carbohydrates into diamonds, food into the muscles, flesh and energy of our bodies. In us such a fire also burns, it constantly transforms air, orange juice, potatoes, bread and meat into useful oxygen, amino acids, lactic acids etc. and then again burning these with the help of oxygen gives off energy which makes us shine, radiating with health and vitality. The wise of India spoke of this process as the 'gastric fire.'

Through the qualities of Fire i.e. illumination, insight and understanding, we can transform hatred and anger into love; t**his transforming power of light has been called 'love,'** numerous stories about the life of saints and sages bear witness. The story of Catherine of Sienna is just one.

In the 14th Century, in the middle of the bubonic plague (which in its first five years killed one third of the European population), a daughter was born to a craftsman, the twenty-third child of twenty-five born to her parents. She was a tiny, charming child; when six years old, she walked with her brother and suddenly saw the sky open and before her sat Jesus, magnificently *dressed in radiant light*. As she stood and stared at the sight, her heart opened towards the radiant source of love.

Following this experience she dedicated her life to God. She ate little and withdrew into her room, until she was allowed to join the order of 'Mantellatte' (for the cloak they wore). She followed the command of her God and began nursing the sick and dying. She did not want anybody to know about it, so she went out at night to the houses of needy families where she left gifts or helped in some small way. During this time she had many more visits of her radiant Lord who told her: "It is your duty to love your neighbour as your own self. Help them spiritually and materially at least with your good will if you have nothing else."

Where does a young girl get her strength from? It is said the Lord appeared again to her and reached into her chest, removed her physical heart and replaced it with his own. Catherine later wrote that the Lord had said, "Dearest daughter, I now give you my own heart and forever you must live by it alone." Her service of love to the sick and dying increased and in time she had many visitations from her Lord. She described this time of transition in her diary: 'The One who had kindled in my heart this fire of love, kept fanning it day by day to a more consuming flame... love had grown strong as death, my heart was rent in two, my soul was set free from this flesh, but alas! For how short a time!' Soon the simple girl, who never went to school soon found herself teaching before the great minds of her world including, bishops, popes and kings. Such is the power of divine inspiration. Surrounded by a community that called her 'dolcissma mama' - sweetest mother, she died when thirty three, not long after having written what she simply called 'The Book;' it is 'the dialogue' between her soul and the Lord.

What would it be like, to live in an awareness that constantly perceives everything as light and love, how would we act? How would we feel? How does light taste? How do we dance with it? How do we sleep in that light, that love? What else can there be, when the fire of love burns in us?

We are used to thinking of 'love' as the passionate and possessive feeling towards our lovers, partners, friends, children, dogs, cats, cars, etc. That love is created from wanting to have, hold, dominate -- real love comes free - like sun energy! It gives forgiveness and warmth to a child; compassion and support to a person who needs; it gives friendship to an equal and respect and devotion to those that are older and wiser. When we have love to give, we don't need something in return – we feel content, full - knowing and trusting there is enough! Such 'loving existence' seems forgotten in many contemporary societies and with forgetting it; we starve ourselves of love, the consequences of which are apparent every day.

We, as a society, behave like hungry fire, consuming all in its wake leaving only destruction, then having to die for lack of love. The sun does not stop shining because we are warm enough; it still gives warmth the next day, and the next, ad infinitum. The experience of such abundance brings joy, fills us with **enthusiasm** (Greek: filled with God, interpreted more freely: filled with light). When I picture joy and enthusiasm, my mind's eye sees ***Fireworks***:

- sees an abundance of bursting, sparkling colours thrown against a dark night sky;
- or the abundance of a summer meadow overflowing with poppies, like a Monet picture; or the gurgling, laughter of a small child giving itself to the joy it feels;
- or a song-bird, that sings to its hearts delight, not for an audience, but out of delight;

The fire of our 'earthly love' needs to be fed! Give…not just to those we love, give support, care, guidance, warmth, share your light, etc. When we are 'in love' we do it naturally, we give our time, thoughts and unending attention to the object of our love – and if we stop feeding our love, do not talk, share, write or perform such actions anymore with/for our loved ones - love dies.

The spiritual fire of love, the fire of enlightenment, gets fed by austerities or self-discipline; the fire of spiritual love just like any fire …**needs food;** and that means giving up something that can be transformed. What we have to give up could be as simple as our tea break, or as complex as our Ego or our Life's aspirations. We love children; we give up much time in bringing them up. We give up our own time and interests in order to have jobs, so that we can provide for them. We love nature; we give up destroying the environment. The more we love life itself, people, animals and plants – the easier we can give up our life to serve them. However little or small, however high or low - if we love it, we have to give up something for it, even if it is our fear, anger or hate! That is the nature of things; that is the law of fire!

What are you willing to give up for the fire of divine love? Only through **renunciation,** through giving up something, can the burning transformation take place. This process has been called: **purification.** Metal ore has to give up its association with earth in the melting process so that it can become pure gold.

Learn from the fire to transform baser tendencies.
Learn from the fire how to enjoy life and celebrate.
Learn from the fire to balance and to give...not to take and destroy!
Learn from the fire how to become light

Contemplation of Air

How can we talk about air, we are hardly aware it's there, our- oh so discriminating nose can't smell it, our ever greedy tongue can't taste it; even the sharpest eyes can't see it; air - such an elusive substance!

This is the very point. The first three Elements are relative "solid", tangible; easy to observe, but air seems in a different category. Indeed in the early Vedic tradition (and others around the world) we find mainly these three Elements – Earth, Water and Fire. Observable there is a marked difference between the "lower" three and the "upper two" Elements; sometimes the upper two have even different names (albeit their characteristics are remarkably the same). According to Sankhya, the gross energy called Air is the penultimate element of creation and dissolution, Space being the most subtle. Children, with minds still less trained in observation and abstraction, think that there is nothing around us - having no awareness or concept of this elusive substance – and yet it's the substance that **connects us** with all other things.

Imagine if the air were yellow!

Just stop reading for a moment, follow your yellow breath. We can't fail to recognize - what was a minute ago air in your child/partner/friend is now in you; the air that was a moment ago inside the cat, a cow or a bird - is now part of you! Suddenly our whole perception has to change - we 'see' that we are connected to everything else - outside and inside, connect (on a gross level) via the air we breath. This connectivity is not static, but in constant movement: breath inside, outside, inside…outside. Repeated movement, rhythm, connects all life. It is not surprising that this

Element is associated in many cultures with communication.

In the Chinese Tradition this 4th Element is called Metal, one reason lies in just this aspect: communication. Its association with 'Metal' becomes clear if we remember how semi-conductors, copper wires etc. are a vital ingredient of instruments of communication.

Here some strange thoughts:
-When Air is compressed/ cooled, it solidifies with substantial weight (becomes ice/ Metal). Metal on the other hand is easy to melt and although not gaseous, it becomes liquid; so both substances span the spectrum, from solid to fluid, gross to subtle.

-When melting down metal, various substances are separated out. The rubbish of the ore floats away, leaving the pure metal; similarly when air gets heated in the lungs, the rubbish of other gases such as nitrogen is breathed out, leaving the pure oxygen for the body to use.
-On a winter's day, or a clear crisp morning, air seems to cut into your lungs - such sharpness is associated with a metal implement, such as a knife/sword!
-Metals naturally occur as a mixed substance, ore! Air is a mixture of gases.

This might suffice to show that there might be similarities in what appears as vastly different, keeping in mind that different cultures have different ways to express themselves. The form changes; the content remains the same.

However let's stay with the use of 'Air' for describing the fourth Element, the fourth field of vibrating energy; let us experience and contemplate this illusive Air. Take a minute, sit up straight, relax your mind and breathe in.

Note the coolness in your nostrils; breathing in more air, feel how your ribs expand, then how your belly fills up. Become aware that air has volume, it expands your body. When the lungs are fully filled, then for a fraction of time there is stillness, then the ribs sink, the lungs deflate and the substance passes through your nostrils again. This time we can feel the warmed air - the substance has changed. If you are sensitive, you might feel a rush of energy through your system, the air intake has changed you!

The original air we took in, consisted of oxygen, small quantities of carbon dioxide and a lot of nitrogen and other rare gases (neon, helium, krypton, radon etc.) and loads of water. Only some of this is kept and used. The air we breathe out contains approx. 5 % less oxygen and an increased amount of carbon dioxide (0.04% to 4%).

The consistency of air changes with every breath a living being man or microbe takes on this planet. We take out mainly oxygen, plants mainly take out carbon dioxide; microbes mainly take out nitrogen (converting it into proteins). Thus **by responding to others, air constantly changes.**

What actually happens when we breathe? There is always some air in the lungs and into this reservoir, a wave of 500 ml of air rushes with every breath, mixing with the old and the new. Imagine the lung as a tree: the trunk as the throat; the bronchioles the main branches, the alveoli are the leaves on the tree, which are surrounded by blood vessels that bring de-oxygenated blood. The higher pressure of the oxygenated blood makes it seep through the walls of the blood vessels, (descending into the lower pressure area); blood then transports it to wherever the body needs it. On the reverse journey, the pressure of carbon dioxide is higher in the blood vessels than in the alveoli - so it seeps through from vessel to alveoli in order to return to be breathed out.

What we perceive as in-breath, change, out-breath - is really no two sudden or distinct things, there is no distinct 'change' at all, but a sequence of small movements. Its continuity in movement! (Note: teachings of the Himalayan Tradition emphasizes – no breaks, no jerks in breathing, but awareness of one continuous flow)

'Change' does not happen all at once, it is a process of a chain of minutely small movements. Hence in Ayurveda, the main characteristic of **this Element is Movement!**

Movement where little bits are continuously left behind! 'Change' happens as a fluid pattern, a rhythm. What we originally saw as "big change", turns out to be an implicit **reoccurring process of leaving behind,** (like a mountaineer leaves the valley behind- although climbing to the peak or: ore leaves debris behind when it becoming molten gold).

This Movement, or **wave of change** and interaction, goes through the many layers of Air, which we call the atmosphere. The first layer is the troposphere; here air becomes increasingly thinner, so that on high mountains, there is barely enough oxygen in the mixture for us to breath, and it gets increasingly colder.

The next layer, the stratosphere has even thinner air and contains a special layer of oxygen called the ozone layer. As one layer merges into the next (stratosphere to ionosphere, to exosphere) the air thins out so much, that eventually where the earth's atmosphere becomes space, only a few molecules of hydrogen and helium float about.

Air has changed so much, it loses its identity!

The strata vary and change depending on the time of year, latitude and activity of the sun and so on. Warm air nearer the earth raises and cools as it moves up and away. In this way Air is constantly on the move; and in many cultures almost synonymous with 'Movement.' In Tibetan and Ayurvedic medicine, this Element is, not surprisingly called "Wind".

Let's look closer at these Wind-movements.
Most frequently we experience the move of Air as a **gentle touch** – but in storms, tornados and hurricanes, it becomes a brute force. (Air, like each of the elements, has an enormous scale!) As we look at a world map, we can see a pattern of obvious rhythmic movements. In the Southern Hemisphere, the 'Trade Winds' follow a certain pattern triggered by the flow of the 'Westerlies' (other winds). In the Northern Hemisphere the swirls of the Northern 'Trade Winds' (Monsoon) determine our summer and winter weather. They work like clockwork: for half a year, they blow from the North-east, the other half from the South-west. Unfailingly in June they bring rain to countries such as India. The '**burst'** of the monsoon can be forecast from year to year almost to the exact day.

We might experience air, not only through its volume (expansion of lungs) and rhythmical movement, but also via its weight. A bucket full of air weighs about as much as two sheets of A4 paper, but consider the height of the atmosphere, then you will realize that a heavy weight is on your head (at sea level 15 lb. on every square inch) - why do we not get squashed? We always have air inside us to create counter pressure. As the weather changes, the atmospheric pressure changes and so does the pressure on our head! (Headaches!)

It seems obvious that **change and movement** belong together, they give a constant **rhythm of renewal and 'good byes'**; a rhythm of creation and dissolution. Marcus Aurelius (Roman emperor and stoic philosopher 121-180 AD) writes:

> Is anyone afraid of Change?
> Why? What can take place without change?
> Can you take a bath, unless the wood undergoes change?
> Can you be nourished unless food undergoes change
> Can you not see, that for yourself also, to change is just
> the same, and equally necessary for the universal nature?

The movement of Air is by no means erratic, as we have seen by 'the winds,' it follows certain patterns: from warm to cold, from higher density to lower density, from in-breath to out-breath, etc. It moves in never-ending, smaller and larger cycles. The cycle of breathing is a relative small cycle - but if we remember that all life breathes - we understand there is 'breath within the breath,' continuity in cycles within cycles! Each breath takes only what it needs, our lungs only absorb as much oxygen as we need – the rest is passed on for others to use what they need. We can't take more breath than we can use nor can we exist with less than we need - this is being **responsible.** Response-ability means, we have to be conscious, to see, observe, be aware of the needs of ourselves, others, of situations and the environment and we have to respond appropriately. To respond appropriately means to act adequately to the situation as a whole, not to react according to my own wants and wishes.

Action not re-action is appropriate to a certain situation. If, for example we breathe in more than we should, we hyperventilate, our body system gets defunct. The same applies on many levels: if we take more electricity than the kettle needs, we burn a fuse; if we use more resources of our environment, it too will "dry up" etc. Responding to our body's, family's or society's need, means taking appropriately - no more! Much of the world's ills, such as pollution (including radioactive and chemical pollution) is the death of our 'green lungs' (the forests of the world). All come from ignoring this principle. Ignoring it makes us ill, poisons body and mind! Inappropriate wanting drives to inadequate response. Even if our body says, 'I need rest' or 'I am full,' we drive it into ever more stressful situations, because our mind decides we need another fridge, car, house, business, lover etc.? Air teaches us to act towards each situation, with **knowing, with intelligence!**

Within the above, hides another 'teaching'. The three lower energy-fields (Earth, Water, Fire) are in their grosser aspects, more related to simple animalistic survival instincts; the subtler elements (Air and Space) echoes a change of awareness. The higher vibrations encourage the search for higher goals hence echo the teachings of Yoga, seeking right knowledge, right behaviour etc. With this our mind turns to the Yamas and Niyamas (Patanjali's Ashtanga Yoga). We seek to practice ahimsa, the wisdom of enough… the wisdom of appropriate response, of response-ability etc.

The trouble is we are not sure what it means 'to act responsibly'. Often we equate it with fulfilling expectations of others, expectations of meeting standardised (or even internalised) requirements of a certain culture, family or person. Appropriate action follows the invite of a unique moment to respond in a unique way; it comes from a point of freedom and love; is **always Now!** Calcified patterns mean we have handed over our power to follow somebody else's decision!

In all this, one aspect is frequently forgotten: we have **responsibility to ourselves!**

- If I do not rest or feed my body adequately, I will be too sick or weak (to look after my child/ job/ family).
- If I do not recognise the passage of time (puberty, old age etc…) the powerful motivation to do, to achieve, to strive will harm (exhaust) our body. We need to recognise when new laws apply!
- If drastic outside events happen (severe illness or death) we need psychological or spiritual appropriate responses.

We need to recognise these changes and act appropriately; this includes how we treat death. Death is part of life, it needs to be understood, talked about and the knowledge of the body's mortality needs to be embraced; that is the demand of the soul. This includes recognising and allowing grief. (Grief is connected to 'letting go', is the emotion of the Air Element.) If we don't take care of these needs of body, mind and soul those vital changes in life will cause problems, our neglect will damage us, poison us. They will "clog the drains", upset the wheels of Change!

Yes, responsibility has its point of reference always **in the Now,** neither being caught up with the past (let go!) nor of the future (don't worry), but act appropriately to the situation now! Only when you are strong you can help others, your strength comes from being present in the here and now and that means including taking care of your own needs.

There still is more: **adequate response to the moment depends on trust**. Trust that there will be air again for the next breath, that there will be enough food!

But if we do not let go of the first breath, we cannot find out, we suffocate with the previous breath. (Problem of asthma) We have to let go and trust there will be more, that there will be help coming at the right moment, that there is always a new cycle of change coming. Because this change is the nature of life, **to trust is to know life**. To understand the movement of life is to live in Trust.

Looking at the cyclic nature of breath, another insight is revealed: Cyclic means it comes again and again! Just like we celebrate our birthday again and again; the sun turns at her highest point again and again etc. Such reoccurring events and behaviour become rituals. The ritual follows a certain stimulus just as the winter cold comes on the back of certain easterly winds. "Ritual" than reminds us to celebrate the underlying connection. Insight into regular reoccurrence is what has led the Element of Air to be associated with **ritual (**Rita; Sanskrit for cosmic law). Air teaches us to listen, to observe re-occurring patterns; they are **cosmic laws revealing universal Truths.** Rita and Satya (Truth) are two sister attributes of the Element Air.

Truth is probably the most elusive aspect of Air. Because of Air's clear and transparent nature, it defines objects clearly. Look at a clean sharp sky, when the air is pure and reveals stars with precision! The landscape appears cut, revealing sharp contours. Air is so clear only when impurities, dust particles, have been 'washed out.

Having spent some time in Rishikesh, which lies in a "dip" in front of the Himalayas, and moreover by the banks of the river Ganga, I observe how the Air is often filled with dust and polluting particles. Why, because the Air is still, trapped....Once there is wind and even more so if there is wind and rain, the Air literally gets washed...and the result is amazing, suddenly the foggy, grey veils that hide the mountains disappear and a clear view reveals their closeness, one can almost see each branch on the trees right up the slopes!

Suddenly the world is clear and the Truth of the mountains is revealed. What has changed is the Air itself, it has been washed; Clarity results! When the Air is clear, life-force is strong, light radiates.

Cornwall my previous home, is famous for its artists' colonies, why? Because the Air is so clean, the light so brilliant and clear that it attracted artists since hundreds of years. The Air is so clean that species of algae and plants grow here, that have been extinguished in many parts of the world. Purity of life and light reveals Truth.

In our minds, this 'washing' process happens through the tools of the intellect; by using **discrimination** - illusions and delusions (the pollution of the mind) are rinsed out, cut away. Under the **power of discernment,** wisdom and truth, the good and pure get separated from what is coarse and primitive. Truth is revealed!

What is this elusive 'truth'? Most people would say: 'truth' is that: Water is wet! 1 km equals 1000 m! Sure all this is 'true,' yet: Water to a fish does not feel wet at all; and 1 km is 0.621 miles! It depends how something is phrased; such kind of 'truth,' even 'scientific truth,' is relative; it changes according to the viewpoint, the times one lives in, the state of science. It changes because life changes.

And yet we argue endlessly whether something or somebody is right, whether this or that is true. Air alerts us, to see, that when we look for every-day truth, we actually look for somebody who looks through the same 'glasses' as you! So **be alert and stop pretending** is the first step to truth! Use discrimination and wisdom to stop seeing what you want to see - or not seeing what you don't. Take off the glasses that condition how you see!

For example: We reassure people they are all right, because we are afraid of their anger. Or, we savour unhappiness, because it assures us people's pity; thus we do not have to change ourselves. Many examples could be given; we are geniuses in masking the truth; we have an enormous talent to self-righteously fool others and ourselves to avoid using our mind to face the truth. We are, in other words, masters of delusion. We cling to our pet projections as though they were gold. It is this delusion that we have to cut away with the **sword of wisdom** in order to see clear. (Note: sword of wisdom/metal/Manjushri's sword…) It is this, which the Element of Air encourages.

However self-inquiry is not an endless mud-raking that pushes waste from one point to another – Air is clearly asking us to face our tendencies such as delusion, blaming, infatuation, laziness etc. and… let them go! But it seems we don't want to!

Lord Krishna had a conversation with one of his disciples about the nature of suffering. The disciple asked the teacher: why do you not change the world - take all people into heaven? Lord Krishna answered that people do not want to go! He asks the disbelieving disciple to find out for himself, and ask whomever he meets. So the disciple goes for a walk; the first Being he meets is a pig. He asks,

"Oh, Pig, if you knew a beautiful garden, a heavenly place would you leave your miserable existence as a pig?"

The pig said, "Sir, will I find refuse and filth and swill there to eat?"

"No," says the disciple, "but you will have food that is extremely delicious and a big garden to play in."

The pig answers: "What could possibly taste better than garbage, what garden could be more wonderful than this mud in which I wallow all day with my young ones? No sir, I am not interested in your heavenly place."

The disciple returned to his teacher, who awaited him with a knowing smile.

The truth is, we do not want to clean up our act; we do not want to move on; how incredible!

Finally, let's contemplate one more aspect of Air. Imagine you are sitting in a garden and you become aware of the Air as a moving substance around you (not unlike water). Imagine you could see this substance. In the warm summer breeze you observe air coming to you, parting to flow around you, then continuing through the garden. It comes to a few hydrangea bushes, lifts up a bit and swirls down again taking a few dry leaves with it! Your garden is on a slope and the Air-flow increases its speed and it takes a bit of dust and dry earth with it, as it hits the windbreak to your vegetable patch. There it gathers its strength, rises up and the momentum takes more leaves; then Air lifts over the windbreak, pushing hard against the bushes. The effort rips more leaves off, even little twigs swirl and dance with them in the back-flow behind the windbreak. As soon as air is back on even ground, it drops the debris!!!!

It continues as though nothing has happened. As air moves, it constantly touches and picks things up! Then it lets go of what it has gathered! At times, this might take some effort but Air has no alternative; it is in its nature to move, picking up and letting go! In this way Air is forever ready to change, it reacts appropriately, then let's go!

The big lesson Air teaches us here is: to live according to what is required in the moment, to act without preconception, without arrogance, to learn to respond clearly and spontaneously without being attached to our past clutter; then we become truly alive, in the NOW. When being ever present, there is no need to cling to the past loves, hates, concepts, ideas of ourselves and others, no need to hide behind our delusions. We take from the world what we need in the moment to sustain life, rather than constantly feed our desire to have even what we do not need.

If we can learn from Air, we can let go of our worries that entice us to armour ourselves, build walls of safety for imaginary protection. For the walls we build to keep us safe, equally keep energies of love and help, even 'the universe' out! We become lonely! Air teaches us to 'ride the wave of change,' let go!

We have this habit of keeping anything of the past on our shoulders and keep it, it weighs us down, and it limits us. We learn something we stick to it and think we have arrived; whether it is a skill, an idea or a religious conviction. We get hold of something and then cling to it "for better or worse", for "dear life". The Mother (re: Sri Aurobindu/Pondicherry) points out that this slows down our development: "Once you have passed through a stage, drop it, let it go! Move on! " How can we evolve if we don't move on? Drop the debris, just as the garden breeze drops leaves.

Meister Eckhardt, prominent mystic, prophet, feminist and philosopher writes in his theology (via negativa) of a path that he calls, 'letting go and letting be.'

When one has learned to let go and let be
Then one is well disposed
and he or she is always in the right place whether in society or solitude
But if one has the wrong attitude
one is always in the wrong place, whether in society or not.
Now one who is rightly disposed, has God within one -
in actual fact in all places, just as much in the street

and in the midst of many people
as in church, or desert, or monastic cell.

Even man's highest goal - his union with God - is dependent on this one principle. So why are we so afraid of letting go, of change? Life changes anyway… it cannot be any different!

'For the will to be free, it needs to let go
and return to its prime origin.
For the intellect to be free it must become naked and empty
by letting go to return to its prime origin.
Think of the soul as a vortex or whirlpool and you will
understand how we are to sink eternally from negation, to
negation … from letting go, to letting go, into God.'

What do we learn from the Air Element?
Movement and change: we learn from air how to appropriately respond. For that we need to cultivate Trust into cosmic order. Clarity: We learn from Air, that clarity reveals Truth. For that we need to cultivate discrimination. Air challenges us to cut away all that is false, unnecessary debris. Let go of what is not needed on all levels, gross and subtle. This is renunciation; on the level of the mind - this is cultivating Silence.

Contemplation of Space

The elusive subtle nature of the fifth Element – SPACE - is mirrored in the many labels it has been given, in different cultures around the globe; however, its meaning remains pretty much the same. It is named Ether/Faith (in some Indian contexts); Wood (Chinese), Nature (African), Great Spirit (American Indian), and Cosmic body of Christ (Medieval Europe). "SPACE" is a widely accepted and most contemporary label, we will work with that. All the labels try to capture three aspects:

- The subtle state of this Element
- Its importance as life's essence and
- Its source in/as the Mystery of the Divine.

These will reveal their knowledge in due course, first just a few thoughts to each "label"; however as the reader will find, they all contain all three aspects:

Ether, according to the Hutchinson Encyclopaedia, is either a colourless, volatile inflammable liquid used, for example, to sterilize and clean wounds - or a hypothetical concept introduced to explain some of the properties of light (Christiaan Huygens).

Some links seem stranger than fiction: ether as cleansing agent! The liver and its organ network is the cleaning agent in the body and in Chinese Medicine and Ayurveda, linked with the energy-field (Element) we have called SPACE.
Furthermore the word Ether in Ayurveda has associations such as: "sound" or "root" "radiation" and "that which does not provide resistance." The latter comes close to the first of the above points, the subtle qualities.

Space, as "that which provides no resistance" is filled with light. This idea reaches deep into spiritual realms of "faith". Samnkhya (Yoga Philosophy) one of the oldest sources of qualifying the energy in five elements, at times uses "faith" to denote that subtlest energy-field, which fills us with light.

Wood, the next label relates obviously more to the second point, the biological life-force, (just as "**Nature**" – and both are symbolically represented as **tree**.) The subtle essence of a tree is its sap, its all-pervading life-force.

The third group of names abstracts even further focusing exclusively on the intangible essence or **Spirit**.

Several ancient traditions talk of the tree of life; a symbol which seems to marry all three aspects: Wood (subtle energy, life-force and Spirit). According to Sankaracharya, one of the most respected ancient philosophers of India, there is - **a botanical tree (Pipal tree, Ficus Religiosa)**, which has been chosen to "represent the entire cosmos, because of its creative meaning;" it is called *Aswattha.* (Sanskrit A – *swattha*) means "that which will not remain the same till tomorrow"; in other words, the tree indicates the ephemeral, ever-changing world of phenomena that rise and dissolve.

In the Bhagavad Gita (Chapter 15) this tree is described as having its roots "up" in space, in the most subtle dimension "that contains all phenomena," and deriving its sustenance *from Beyond.* Its leaves and branches speak of spiritual growth and the knowledge that leads to a noble life, enabling the knower to reach Self-realisation. The plurality of worldly existence, including the human experience, is allegorically pictured as a fig tree arising from - and sustained by, higher energies; even consciousness.

Space is that potential, that womb "which gives accommodation to all things" (Sanskrit: *Akasa);* it represents and holds the knowledge, the blue-print of all phenomena; in its pure state it is consciousness. I like the symbol of the American Indians: a Blanket! Each culture, each tradition of referring to this fifth, subtlest element, reveals a different corner of the same blanket!

So let's contemplate what we can learn from the Chinese, who use the symbol **'Wood'**: Imagine a majestic tree standing on a mountain-top; spreading its branches in all directions, - it has a commanding view, allowing an extended vision. Space provides us with superior vision, enabling us to see beyond illusion.

- A tree (as well as man), exposed to all weathers, being pulled by winds this way and that, must be firmly rooted! Two teachings hide in this: a tree bends this way and that in the wind, but can do so only because it is firmly rooted. We too weather the many storms of life, if our roots are firmly planted, in that which ultimately nurtures us.

- When roots are loose, the sap blocked or the vision limited, the tree cannot fulfil its dharma (its being-ness). The sap of life cannot rise, stunting growth. Such a tree withers and dies; out of congestion, illness arises!

- To heal the rising sap has to be strong enough to find new ways of expressing life, cleaning the blockages, freeing itself from restrictions and relaxing back into the original task. The latter is synonymous with surrendering to the all-embracing principle of higher unity, where we become part of a multi-dimensional living organism.

- Trees have a unique feature, called geotropism. Normally trees grow upwards; they grow towards the light. I remember a narrow valley in the Grampians of Australia where the trees grew horizontally, at a 45 degree angle to the slopes instead of straight up, in order to reach the little light that was let into the centre of the canyon. Wood always stretches *towards light – and against gravity.* The dynamism between light and gravity is pregnant with meaning in most modern physics, but there is no "space" to go into that here. Just note that a tree also grows *towards the force of gravity*; they have a special ability to tune into the earth's magnetic field with their roots; thus *a* ***tree stretches in two opposite directions,*** **or into all directions (re: multi-dimensional space.**

- Trees stem from seeds (ancestors), producing seeds; they are "parent-plants." The seed contains a complete blueprint of what its fruit is going to be. No cabbage seed has ever grown into a bushel of rice. The seed with its inherent plan - or its morphogenetic field - is put into the ground *carrying its karma*. There the earth protects it, so that it can germinate. For this process to begin, the environment has to be just right for that individual seed in order to make the quantum leap from seed to seedling. For some plants it takes days, for others decades, for some it takes fire (to crack open seed-pods), for others water; for some it takes sand, for others rich humus. Why and how these needs are shaped, depends not only on the environment for which they are destined, but is also on the blue-print they carry, the knowledge inherently held. (This collective knowledge held is referred to as cosmic knowledge, eternal knowledge or sometimes the Akashic records).

The seedling has a special relationship to its environment; the conditions for its development are crucial. Initially it has its own potential to grow roots (a measure of wholeness and independence), but soon the seedling requires dependence on others i.e. sunshine, rain, nutrients in the ground, shade, wind, adequate space etc. (it has to establish links between its inner needs and the outer world). Once a young tree, it further needs to respond to its environment with flexibility, needing to bend in strong winds, otherwise the high demands could snap the trunk. To remain flexible it needs adequate water to dissolve the nutrients provided by the earth and to fill the cells with sap, hence its dependency on water. Without water it will dry out and shrivel up or break at the next encounter with wind, animal or man. When dry it easily falls prey to fire.

Some trees, old and sturdy trees like the Redwoods, and Mahogany, can actually survive fires not only while green and living, but also when dried up, or cut. The reason lies in the density of their cell structure, which does not allow the oxygen the fire needs, to penetrate. One could say these are so strong in their integrity, so true to themselves, their "tree-ness" and conviction, that nothing can touch them. Some of these trees are three thousand years old!! Branches can be cut off, the trunk be sawn off, and still the sap is so strong that it makes new growth, new shoots, eventually a new tree. It helps a young tree to grow up in a group; they provide shelter for each other.

But eventually some will outgrow this arrangement, needing more space. **Trees compete for space and light**. If they have not enough they wither. Let us assume our young tree survived and his companions made room for him, then it grows stronger with each season. His branches will stretch in many directions, some bigger, stronger, longer, some smaller, shorter, weaker. Some of these branches will die. In the winter, the sap will retreat to the centre of the trunk, or the roots, to avoid the frost. In order to prevent severe damage, the sap retreats, avoiding a damaging confrontation with icy winds or drying frost. This withdrawal from the harsh winter attacks might lead to branches dropping off, yet as long as the centre stays untouched, "unimportant" shoots can be sacrificed. **The tree renounces aspects of lesser importance while maintaining faith and trusting that spring will come** again; or that after a dry period it will rain; or in the case of endless rain, that the sun will shine again. The tree stands, **observes, is detached!** *(Just see the parallel, does Space ever get involved in what happens in it?)*

And when spring comes, the tree's faith is rewarded. With confidence and vigour he produces new shoots, leaves, branches, flowers and fruit - only to withdraw again in the autumn into himself to integrate last summer's experience. In this way, he grows stronger as long as he maintains enough flexibility to sway in the wind, yet stays firmly rooted in the ground. This says something about measured existence, not wanting what cannot be yours! Accepting life as it is.

In this way his roots grow too, reaching deep, like the anchor of a ship, while his crown reaches high into the sky *(bridging the gap between micro-and macro-space)* with a canopy of leaves that soak up the sun and rain. Once old and established, he has a beautiful vista over wide rolling hills, a view over life as it proceeds, unattached, contained and peaceful.

His peace is by no means egotistic; he gives generously and selflessly to others. Even though the earth and environment provide for his needs, in exchange he gives oxygen, life-sustaining energy abundantly, to all that live. Generosity is one of his characteristics, for not only does he give oxygen (vital *prana*) to others, but eventually sacrifices himself to fire. But all along he gives small necessary gifts to those friends that need, providing a community for others. All sorts of animals and birds live in his branches, live in him or off him; he supports plenty of life unperturbed.

The tree can protect others throughout blizzards, droughts and floods because his roots are firmly planted and his energy is self-contained; he is not bothered by little guest creatures (from bug to bird), they live according to their nature, as he does to his. He is detached from the things going on in and around – may be even grateful, for their droppings are of some benefit, fertilizing his earth. He might even share his version/vision of life with them.

One day the woodcutter comes and decides it is time to cut the tree. It takes the tree trunk a long time to dry out; the wood is ready to be used again! The natural beauty of the tree is still recognized; its spirit, its legacy, can still be appreciated and enjoyed by people who own the wooden furniture for hundreds of years. Yet some of the tree will be cut into logs and burned in the fireplace; but then the tree always was aware that it carried fire intrinsically in himself. In its wisdom, Wood knew and accepted that finally transformation comes into pure energy, into pure spirit, into light. After all wood is nothing but a storehouse of sunlight; fire returns/ transforms it, to its source: light.

The symbol of "Wood" shows the complexity of light's journey, through the phenomenal world back into its state of origin, pure light. Hidden is a beautiful metaphor of space manifesting out of itself all phenomena, the womb of creation and finally dissolving that very existence. Who would have thought, that a tree or a piece of wood can teach us, the "wisdom of Space"! Indigenous people of many cultures (not just Chinese cultures knew) because they observed and held the tree as sacred for this very reason. In some African wisdom, the tree is the most highly evolved existence, - *not the human being,* for their quality of detachment, their age-old wisdom, and their life- giving and life- sustaining energy.

C**ontemplating Space is much more difficult**? Its vastness seems prohibitive. To talk about space is like talking about infinity - there seems to be no limit for our mind to hold on to; space has no boundaries; it is infinite in place and time. However we make ourselves (scientifically speaking) an artificial horizon by means of light and gravity so that "we can conceive the universe as a container with an edge in which there are moving objects processing information. The edge of the universe is the horizon. It is as far as we can see today ..." (C. Potter, We Are Here).

We call that, cosmic horizon.

This grandness is hard to grasp. Looking at the night sky, we see billions of stars, planets from near and far, and yet whatever we see is, of course, the tiniest fraction of space; it belongs to one family of stars we call the Galaxy!

Recently I heard someone say: "we used to think there were a million galaxies, well these days we know there is a galaxy for every grain of sand on this earth." The nearest Galaxies to us are the two Magellanic Clouds; they are 180,000 light years away! One of the biggest Galaxies that has been studied so far is one called M87; it is a million light years across and 50 million light years away. These numbers go beyond our comprehension beyond even imagination - and that goes too for what goes on in it.

Space - despite its incomprehensible grandness, is still an object of our perception, something we can study, analyse – it is "beyond us" only because of our limited view of reality. On one hand there is the vastness of space – on the other, each grain of sand, each blade of grass is filled with space! There is not just the vastness of the macro-cosmos, but the even more incomprehensible vastness of the microcosm. Every phenomena whether a gas-explosion on the sun, Mars, Jupiter and other planets or a blood-cell in our body, has potential and manifestation **in space and of space.** Less than one billionth of the human body is material; the rest is space!!! This incredible complexity is not without order; stars follow a certain life span, the earth has a certain life rhythm. A plant has a certain structure, as humans, we have a certain life cycle, so does our skin and cells; creation is not chaotic. Richard Dawkins, not without humour, says:

“Nature, it seems is the popular name, for milliards and milliards and milliards of particles playing their infinite game of - billiards and billiards and billiards.”

Space generates out of itself, particles that come together in certain, seemingly innocent objects – and then something happens; the phenomena or object – acquires the ability ‘to self-replicate, the object is able to use the surrounding materials to make exact copies of itself’ (Dawkins) and bingo! We have manifestations. No wonder Space has become the metaphor for infinite complexity of creation, or evolution out of that which exists before …“Space”, even if we can’t comprehend what it actually is - is experienced as the ultimate generative power of all existing phenomena. No wonder we need a simple manifest metaphor alongside it, (such as the tree) to comprehend.

Space does not only contain all that exists, but it contains everything before it exists, as well as all the laws according to which it exists; a matrix for future potential - ad infinitum. It is awesome to think that not only all solid matter, the desk, the chair, the computer all, around me exist in space, but the potential of this article exists in space as “blueprint” even before I write it. Even our future great-grandchildren already exist potentially in space!

It gives a totally new understanding to the age-old argument between predetermination and free will. It suggests that, the potential for all sorts of actions are mapped out, yet don’t forget: all options and all consequences are included! Mind splitting complexity!

The blueprints are there, and we with our will make manifest – yet only that which is already possible. As always: both ‘sides’ of the ancient argument are right! Eastern philosophies have maintained all along, that past patterns (karma) hold present choices.

If space contains not only all matter, but also all potential - then **space contains time,** by virtue of containing the sequence of events between potential and manifestation. It makes Albert Einstein's suggestion of a space-time continuum obvious. Space, that includes time, has not only as we assume in everyday life three, but four dimensions, or as scientists of today have it nth-dimensions. (David Bohm). Space is truly unlimited. Can we stretch our minds to understand and feel the above? Normally we look at objects, see a table and perceive it as a solid object. This way of seeing things, is called in modern physics the middle dimension - the way of everyday life, it is a useful way of looking at things. Yet we know from modern physics that objects are not really like this, they are not only made of small bits of matter, but these atoms consist of many tinier and tinier things or even "strings!" If we imagine one tiny atom of our table to be magnified to be as large as the dome of St. Peter's Cathedral in Rome (the largest Cathedral), we would see that really the atom is huge empty space (just like the Cathedral). In it a grain of salt and a few specks of dust (nucleus and electrons) are flying about! – Wow! (Fritjof Capra)

My hand is really masses and masses of microscopic space filled with a few free floating, minute particles. Wow! Of course mystics have seen this along; their awareness is so finely tuned that they live in this extended awareness; this other dimension is called *turiya*, the "fourth dimension", which reveals the essential emptiness, or the void. *Mahayana Buddhism* accepts this empty space as the true "Body of Being", *Dharmakaya*, ultimate essence – and that is what we are.

In the old *Vedic tradition* too, there is the notion of space as emptiness, *mahakasa* is the great space, where "nothing" exists and simultaneously all exists, divine consciousness. When the focus is not on emptiness, but on consciousness – the source of all potential - then space is called *cidakasa*.

In emptiness, vibration of energy is "motion in space", that is all there is! Now comes the odd bit: what we perceive as the world is only those frequencies which our limited five senses can register and thus deem as existing – to the rest we are "blind!" And yet there is a whole universe of moving energies out there. So to talk about space as such is only referring to that which we can register or imagine; there is much about space, due to human limitations that we cannot qualify, we can't say anything about - Sages call this filled Space. Once pure space is filled, is polluted; it contains the energies that include us! The purity of the innocent space-body is what is described in the Guru Gita (Skanda Purana) Verse 64.

> I am everlasting, self-luminous, taintless and completely pure. I am the supreme Ether. I am immovable, blissful and imperishable.

This is our original nature, to become aware of it and sink into that pure space; in Buddhist and Vedantic traditions it is seen as the bliss of emptiness. To focus on that pure inner Space becomes a tool to unblock and free us from our "complicated, narrow, boring and limited reality." The '*Rishis*' explored the inner space through meditation, and called it *athma bodha*, the house of *Atman/Brahman*. They also knew this must not be confused with the Ultimate itself; it is still an object of observation i.e. still limited by our perception. It is *Akasa* – perceptible, it is that space which contains phenomena, belonging to the *Mahabhuta.*

Space, just as each Element, has this quality of pointing beyond itself to its divine origin: Earth points to the creative goddess, Water reminds us of the flow of life itself. Fire called us to witness the God-light and with Air we are aware of *prana*, the vital essence, breath of life. **Now Space adds the void filled with divine potential,** as we alluded to in the third point at the beginning. With this, Space as well as 'tree,' calls us to expand our perspective beyond place and time:

High upon Sacred Mountain,
With unrestricted view,
The clarity of vision
Comes to us anew. (Jamie Sams)

This expanded vision challenges our intelligence – we have the potential to achieve anything in life! The potential is there before we even take a step, moreover our mind knows, even our brain knows any idea already before we do - yes - and it sends out a message to the body, muscles etc. instructing them what to do. Before action comes knowledge, comes intelligence, comes wisdom. All of nature acts from the source of such innate wisdom. Before setting out to seek a new job, a holiday destination, a new motive to paint, or a new direction in life, really before doing any job, before planning a city, before raising a child - the idea, the vision, is always there. Only once we have this "vision" can we harness our strength and find the right tools to do the job! Only then can others join in and help us to get "where we want to be". Space has in itself the "ideas" even before the start of evolution.

As above so below, we need such vision too. When stuck in life we ask, "What shall I do? Where shall I turn?" What am I supposed to do with my life? In these situations Space offers its wisdom: A lettuce does not produce carrots; similarly each of us has their own potential. **To find our potential, to find the vision that is ours, we have to look into ourselves, into our inner space, to reach the unformed potential, our most powerful source! This process is called meditation. If we quiet our mind, eventually we will hear our own inner wisdom, showing us the right path.**

Different traditions have different ways of doing this. Tribal people, under the guidance of a wise person, are often sent into remote locations, such as a hill top, and asked to pray, fast and meditate for three or four days. In the more urban environment, we might choose to go on a retreat, especially a silent retreat. A businessman, needing an insight into his business deals, might just lock himself in the office for a while. Whichever method we choose to reach our own inner wisdom, we need to know that it can be reached, because it is already contained in space! The question is not *whether* we can access it, but **how to shut out all other interruptions and babbling of our mind, so that we can see the vision, hear the wisdom. This is the path of Yoga.**

The next problem we have is, we do not believe what we hear, we have little faith, do not trust our own wisdom. Space teaches us to respect our own inner wisdom. It is there; call it Higher Self, Soul or Intuition! Inside ourselves, inside our mind we have Space containing all the wisdom we need. With **this inner wisdom-space, we are 'plugged' into the universal Wisdom-Space, universal mind or consciousness**. The guidance will come - we just need to respect it, trust it, and not doubt it.

Space does not doubt itself: “Oh, maybe this oak tree doesn’t look right, maybe I better give it some blue leaves;” Space trusts its integral knowledge, respects its own decision.

Once we have learned to respect our inner wisdom we know that the same is in every being and thing. If inner wisdom is in the Space that is me, how can it not be in the Space that is you? So I need to respect your Space, the tree’s Space, the house’s Space, the earth’s Space etc. Space containing **wisdom, divine wisdom is sacred Space.** Sacred Space needs to be **treated with respect** and awe - have we not seen earlier how awesome space is? Each creature is by nature “sacred Space”; each being needs respect, no matter what kind, creed, shape or colour. Treating these with respect means not to allow others, or yourself, to abuse them in any way, not allow ourselves to violate sacred space:

Treat every-thing, person, animal and plant with respect. Treat every thought, idea, concept, religion, and philosophy with respect. Treat everything, form or formless with respect, it will change your way of being, your whole life! It will affect how we build our cities, how clean we keep our air, whether we have enough room to live – or parks to relax in?

It affects our relationships too - how about our friendships? Are we possessive towards our friends, partners or children? Do we give them enough space, enough distance to do what they feel is right? Do we allow enough support and space for other beings to develop their full potential? If we would give people such quality space they would have no need for drugs, no need for fights and over-reaction, no need even for harmful stress.

Finally: do we give ourselves enough space to relax during the day, sacred space to be with our own inner self to grow emotionally, energetically and spiritually?

Let us summarize: Space/Wood is an energy-field with certain characteristics. **It is all-pervasive, spreading into all directions, known, unknown and yet to be known - including time. It contains an enormous, creative potential generating out of itself all phenomena. It does this with intelligence, holding all phenomena in an ordered way. It contains the door to infinity and is laden with divine intelligence; it's the vehicle that carries Chit (Consciousness) in all existence.**
It calls us to treat every existence as sacred Space.

Element Magic

We have shared some great knowledge about the Five Elements. You might at this junction have come to believe that you understand what the Five Elements are about. What you have read gives you a great insight into that which we know makes up the phenomenal universe. We have looked at each of the Elements in some details and on a scale that shows their many facets and levels.
Let's recap:

There is Earth, the manifest level of creation, the embodiment of solidity, that holds all without judgments. That attracts with its gravity all objects. It is generous and compassionate. It is that which holds within our body and mind all phenomena (food, thoughts, feelings).

There is Water, the fluid element, adapting to any circumstances and nourishing all life. That which stores wisdom and uses willpower and determination, flowing from past to future aiming to reach the ocean (fulfilment of dharma). That which teaches us how to surrender without fear of losing our identity.

There is Fire, that transforms gross to subtle, food to energy and vice versa. That while seemingly destroying one - creates and illuminates another. That which radiates healing light and warmth; heralding joy of life. That which is fuelling the turning-point – towards the light, that we are.

There is Air, the vital breath which is the carrier of the life-force (prana). That elusive element, we feel through its movement and respond. That which is transparent, bringing clarity and knowledge of the cosmic order. That encourages to discriminate and let go of all that which clouds.

And there is Space, all-pervasive, timeless, spreading from known to unknown; containing the creative potential, that generates all phenomena. It contains the door to infinity and is laden with divine intelligence. Carrying Chit (Consciousness) in all existence, making it sacred Space.

So we have, as previously mentioned, five energy fields, with **distinctly different flavours.** Well, let's look closer; let's take a microscope:

Imagine a stone; it is obviously solid, obviously belonging to the energy-field we called Earth. Hm? But then imagine you visit that stone again, in say 20 000 years, and it has become sand which flows like water through your hand, adapting to the vessel you pour it into – and you might become aware that that is actually a description of the Water Element! Yes!

Now go back another 20 thousand years and the very stone is molten lava; obviously Fire.

Holding the stone in your hand, now, - take a microscope and look at the stone and you will discover there are tiny pockets of Space filled with Air. In fact a scientist would say the stone is 70 % Space. **So what *appears* as Earth, a clearly established energy-field, actually consists out of Five different elemental qualities;** meaning: all five are inherently present in the stone (albeit we can only appreciate them with the aid of time).

Not convinced? Let's take Water.
Open your fridge and go to the ice-compartment. Take an ice-cube. It's obviously solid, manifest, characterized by the most significant description of the Earth element. While you hold it in your hand, it melts…and turns obviously into water. What turns ice into Water is the warmth of your hand, is Fire! Water is only water and not ice, because of the presence of Fire! If you know the chemistry of water, you know that oxygen is one of its main chemical properties; apart from the fact, that water has no colour and is clear and transparent… just like Air! We could say it obviously occupies Space, but we can even go further and say, water evaporates and its finest form is ascending high into Space, becoming part of Space. In fact, we breathe water…not just air…but that will confuse you even more!

Let's take a third example:
Think of a flame. It burns because there is something combustible, something solid to burn. In the case of a tame flame of a candle it is the wick. There is no fire, without that "solid" wick, so there is no Fire without Earth. From a scientific level we could say the process of combustion gives of water...hey that's how our fireball (earth) turned into oceans! Yes; but we can be much simpler and just look at the flame as it moves and flows from one form into another... the major quality of Water! - Fire transforms the wick; the burning process itself transforms the wick into ashes, giving off heat and light...obviously Fire! Fire cannot burn without Air, as any school-kid knows; obviously the flame exists in Space, in-fact the light of the flame in ever subtler phases radiates into infinite Space.

What is this? We understood there were Five energy fields, now it seems that each of these five fields contain each other. Yes, and it gets even more intriguing: Just one easy example! *Take the wick of the candle, which is " the earth of the Fire",* it has substance, (Earth) it has inherently the flow of dissolution of time (Water) it has inherent the capacity to be transformed (Fire) it has air-pockets trapped between its fibres or molecules (Air) and it occupies Space. So we can talk of the **Space in the Earth in the Fire,** of the wick. **And this is so ad infinitum... in ever subtler, on ever less perceptible levels.**

Each Element contains each Element!

I visualize it, as though looking through a kaleidoscope at an Element. When we do, we look at one thing, but see it refracted and refracted again and again. In fact science talks about fractals, (self-repeating) and about the universe having symmetry as one of its original powers. In one of the scriptures, the Vivekachudamani it says: Having united with parts of one another, they (the Elements) become gross and become the cause for the formation of the gross body…" The theory that explains how these have "grossified" is called *Panchikarana…*'(Swami Chinmayananda) Through self-duplication and mutual combination, each gross element ends up consisting ½ of its own character (say Air), one eighth borrowed from ether (space), 1/8th of Fire, 1/8th of Water and 1/8th of Earth. Thus each of the five Gross Elements is a combination including all other elements. (Panchadasi, Sudhanshu Chaitanya; Chapter I).

Meaning: Air is 50% determined by its own energy, but in addition has some Element of Space (occupies space), some part of Fire (moves), has some characteristic of Water (is transparent) and Earth (consists of solid molecules, has weight). **Because each Element contains all others, it can never stay still; always interacting, it changes into the variety of phenomena we perceive as the ever-changing world.**

Although constantly in flux, constantly changing, we perceive it in one form, because at each particular moment in time, one Element is dominant. It means, that if we look deep enough, that which appears as Five succinct Elements, is intricately connected; making such a complex, many dimensional Web, that they become indistinguishable from each other; hence they merge, they are ONE (with no particular distinction…(nirguna) or all particular distinctions as potential to be expresses (satguna).

We have in fact looked at the un-foldment from the ONE

into the many, from the opposite side than what we usually do. Normally we explain how the ONE Ultimate (whatever you call it) unfolds through various steps into the Mahabhutas, the Five Gross Elements and with that into the plurality of forms. Above we have turned the telescope (the magnifying glass) the other way.... Because normally we see the immense plurality in our phenomenal world and at best perceive the five fields, but when we look towards their source these merge in such infinite complex Webs (many dimensions, many possibilities) so much so, that the interconnectedness of all possibilities makes the differences disappear into their potential.

This is what the physicist David Bohm might have described as n^{th} dimensions. It's like standing on the beach. You feel the water around your feet, there is a beautiful little wave curling against your toes...your focus is on just this little beautiful wave: one element. You lift up your eyes and you see a few more, say "Five Waves" (five Elements) ....**then look at the horizon and what you see is one body of water. All differences disappear;** the five Elements are only there under limited focus; (the phenomenal world, bound by our limited perception). **BUT in the phenomenal world they are very real and helpful.** This is how it is with the diversity of phenomena we experience.

In this diversity, the Five Elements are a complete and very useful concept; a grid to help us see and understand the world, our lives, relationships, bodies and our health etc.
They help us to see clearly; to be mindful and balanced. But we need to keep the awareness that these five forms, in ultimate complexity merge into each other, merging and emerging in and from ONE.
They are *not really separate*, as we saw. They are in total

connectedness; nothing exists separately. The great illusion we live in is, that anything exists separately from the rest!

Worse "Tom-foolery", we experience it as though it is. Why? Because of our perception (only seeing the little wave playing around our toes).

Now we see them, now we don't! That is magic!
Can you hold both as Truth? Then you can work with these, in the phenomenal world to whatever complexity and subtlety your personal mind is capable of.

We need concepts to understand our world, our lives, ourselves, but in the end we need to be aware that concepts are still concepts! Concepts are not Absolute Truth, they are tools, filters; filters that simplify and enable us to live in this phenomenal world. The five Elements are filters for our human instruments of perception. This is meant when in Sankhya (Yoga Philosophy) it says that the tanmatras: seeing, hearing, touching, tasting, smelling **exist before** …the awareness of the manifest world, the Five Elements.

So what can be understood? The elements are real…and they are not real! Nonsense…or Magic?

A useful play of our perception, a play that happens according to certain cosmic realities, laws even. Like standing by the ocean and looking at the horizon - unaware of waves, we see just water. The horizon of our world/knowledge has in the past moved with the growth of our awareness (From flat earth to round earth; from atoms to neutrinos). Can we "lift our eyes, so that we can see the horizon, where the five fields of energy, we call Elements become ONE – on that horizon we "see" Consciousness.

Can you dare to be aware of Consciousness and see its manifestation in the Great Five? If you do, the wisdom of the Five will unfold within you and be a brilliant guide to life in this dimension, in this phenomenal world of manifest energies, that we call our universe, our planet, our lives, our bodies, our relationships. And that means you may grow to see the beauty of these Five as the expression of the Divine, the ONE, just as **St. Francis of Assisi, with whom we can praise God within the Five Elements:**

> Altissimu omnipotente bon Signore (most highest almighty God…)
> Be praised my Lord, especially Sir brother sun…who takes meaning from you, Most High,…and sister Moon and the stars in heaven.
> Be praised my Lord, through brother wind: through air and every kind of weather, by which you give sustenance to your creatures.
> Be praised, my Lord, through sister water, who is useful and humble and precious and pure.
> Be praised, my Lord through brother fire through whom you illuminate the night, beautiful, joyful, vigorous and strong.
> Be praised my Lord through the sister, our mother earth, who sustains and rules and produces different fruits with coloured flowers and grass….
> *(Brendan Smith; The Silence of Divine Love)*

Through becoming aware of the complex interconnectedness of the Five, we become aware that everything is part of everything else, there is only ONENESS, but One, not as a number, but **One without a second.**

Through whatever magnifying glass (or kaleidoscope) you look at your vision of the Totality, the ONE will be coloured by the very instrument you use.

Contemplating **Earth** the ONE will be honoured as Gaya or Bhumi, or Danu or Anu (Celtic). If you contemplate **Water**, and arrive at the vision of the ONE, you will see and honour That as Poseidon, as Varuna or as the rainbow-serpent (Australian Aboriginals). If you contemplate **Fire**, you will come to honour the ONE as Agni, Surya or Ometeocl or Shantico (Aztec). One with his mind set for contemplation on the **Air** Element, will discover the ONE through Vayu or, dare I say so – the Holy Spirit. One with his eyes on **Space** will discover Shiva and beyond to Parashiva or Kishelamakank (Lenape / Native American) etc. etc.

It means that each Element has inherently the possibility to lead us to the Absolute, but as limited beings we have a predilection to select a certain form. Our visionary language is coloured by whatever culture or society which provides the 'kaleidoscope' through which we look. The more indigenous cultures are frequently focused on Earth, Water and Fire; in more abstract thinking cultures/time the focus is especially on Air/Space. The Vedic culture "sees" especially through the "eyes" of Fire and so Agni plays a major part. As contemplation advances one realises: Fire of course in the subtle aspect is light. Thousands of years of contemplation of the Wise Ones revealed light as the light of Consciousness.

But whatever language we use, whatever lens we use for looking in the 'distance', in the beyond, we look where all differences disappear in ONE. Awareness of this makes all religious bias "colouring".

Contemplating the Elements, eventually leads to going beyond their colouration (colour- Sanskrit: raga) It leads to practice vairagya, detachment; removing our colouring, our opinions.

Through the "looking glass" closely, we discover that the Five Elements reveal their nature as merged in the ONE; i.e. they lose their individual colouring.

BUT coming back to 'Earth" from such lofty heights: Until we can live from that level of insight, the Five Elements are a great tool to increase our awareness, to become mind-full; to learn about ourselves and others on many levels; in fact they can be our greatest teacher- if we let them!

Hence in the Jnana Sindh, Parashiva explains to Kartikeya (one of Shiva's sons) the supreme Guru "All directions, all spaces, all mountains, all forests, all rivers, all oceans, and all great masses of land - **everything formed of the five elements – are the very body of the Guru."**

Let them be our teacher!

Part II

Earth, her season and relationships....

The Earth is usually associated with late summer, in most cultures... However by now we know that "seasons", once we start thinking globally, have less to do with a time of year, than with a quality.

We can look at bare Earth and consider it simply a "clod" of minerals and plant fibre. This "bare earth" can be seen in the temperate regions, when fields are ploughed and resting in winter; and so it comes that some cultures associate winter with earth. Similarly we can see "bare earth" in high mountains; in the dryness of a tropical summer, even in deserts. Such "bare earth" reminds us of strength and the raw power of gravity, which comes from earth's very own core.

A centre is that from which all else takes its reference; such a hub is a powerful still-point. In the Northern hemisphere winter makes us aware of this core-stability which is mirrored in the centre of our physical body, the belly. In some eastern traditions this is called the Hara, or more poetically, "the Triadic Heart of Shiva" (Kashmir Shaivism,). This central part of our body holds two power points (used in Martial Arts and complementary medicine) the "tan tien" and the "Core Star". Both are believed to carry our physical essence; in Yoga we experience the Manipur Chakra as this centre, which holds prana, life-energy. Injury in the belly - the centre, results in serious damage to life and even death (Ritually used in hara-kiri (jap.).

We perceive and act in the world through our subjective

perception; we are the centre of our world. As such we each have a part to play in society, if one neglects that place, if one neglects what is central to one's life, be it health, family, friends, job, values or any basic needs, it will affect one's life's energy. Similarly, on a subtler plane, we are in essence, in our core divine; if we neglect to acknowledge or to live according to this divine centre, it will affect our life adversely. If we don't take care of these centres....on whatever level, we will feel cut loose, uprooted, at odds, restless, frustrated, lonely - a lacking, a craving, but for what? As a reaction we search to fill this "inner void" with substitutes, e.g. work, thinking too much and worrying too much, or feeding the void in the belly with snacks, sweets, sex and turn even to addictions to alcohol and drugs.

If we neglect the earth, which is the root-centre of human existence, life loses its meaning, we feel separate, we act disconnected. We can see the devastating effects of losing our own "intrinsic Earth", as well as our relationship to the Earth across the globe. It is not without reason that the Bible describes man "as made of Earth". To recognise our place on Earth, in society, in the family of sentient beings is the sacred duty and responsibility of each "Earthling".

Within our being this search for our centre culminates in the question which Ramana Maharshi made famous: "Who am I";

This question has occupied wise people throughout: from Buddha to Christ, from Mohammed to the Dalai Lamas, from Shamans to therapists and psychologists, Rishis and Yogis all unite in asking us this central question of our existence. **Who are you? What is your centre?**

To find the answer we have to become like the earth; still... still like a mountain; just there; stable and contained, withdrawing from all distractions. To "become like the Earth," "to be like a mountain" are apt metaphors often used in Zen Practices to describe meditation. "To just sit" with no distractions, no doing, just holding awareness of one's Self is, in many traditions, East and West, is considered "the way to the centre". In that stillness the voice of the Self can be heard. The African Shaman Malidoma Patrica Some writes: "The centre is both within and without. It is everywhere. But we must realise it exists, find it, and be with it, for without the centre we cannot tell who we are, where we come from and where we are going." (Of Water and Spirit; Arkana 1994)

The American Indians tell us we need to find our own drumbeat inside ourselves, the rhythm of Life that is specific to ourselves, yet fits totally into the drumbeat of mother Earth.

The Ismailii community (Moslem) has a manual (written in Pahlavi; from the 4th century), that contains questions and answers for young people. Everybody over fifteen is supposed to know the answer to these questions: "Who am I and to whom do I belong?" "Whence have I come from and whither am I returning?" "What is my proper calling in earthly existence?".

Let's contemplate another angle. At present I am in India, in the season after the monsoon, growth is lush, flowers abound, even the grass is green. **This fullness of "bringing forth" is what many associate with Earth and summer;** i.e. the season of abundant growth after the rains, where the first vegetables are harvested, where fruits of the earth are plentiful; where berries suddenly change colour and are ripe to eat.

Where the wheat turns golden ready for harvest.

When we are aware of HER abundant giving, we too give generously; we can do so because we know there is enough. In that knowing we are content with what we have. This sense of having plenty and having plenty to give characterises the summer as a season as well as a stage of life, and it is captured in the Yogic precepts (Yamas and Nijamas) of "non- stealing, (asteya) and contentment". (Also mentioned in Part I) Non-stealing and contentment express the earth qualities of giving rather than taking. It is this quality of the earth that we have lost in a big way in the modern world! We take…from each other and from the earth herself with an alarming rate…because: "I want!"

At present one third of the world's population uses the available "fruit of the earth and its resources…" leaving 2/3 of the population lacking! That is stealing, in a big way! **That is not honouring the Spirit of the Earth! We exploit the earth to feed our greed,** in innumerable ways. It is of utmost importance for the global society that we learn to live differently. We behave like robbers: we exhaust the earth and then put chemicals on Her body to get even greater yields! We need to learn to farm our lands in such a way as not to want more and more crops out of the ground. But that is only the smallest issue; have you ever seen pictures how we rob the earth of its core in mining, where people work under the most deadly conditions. The investment managers of the big companies say: it's our obligation to make profit; we don't care how! (See the DVD "Let's make money!")

We need to change, need to learn how to be content with less than what we have got! The root of "wanting" is judgment that something is "more valuable, than what I have," From judgment comes want; from want comes "stealing!" Most of the earth's population are guilty of that; **we are not heeding the earth's teaching: "Give... rather than Take". Live simple so our earth does not perish due to our exploitation**.

Despite our greed earth herself gives tirelessly; Hildegard von Bingen (12th, century Woman Saint of Europe) points out: "would the earth not fulfil its task of providing "growing," there would be no air. If the water would not be softening and taming the earth... and the earth not taming the water, and lead it into the right pathways, the water could not have its mirror-like quality that points to the depths... (Heilkunde, H. von Bingen)

A person who is dominated by the quality of earth-energy is serving diligently – her family, or may be as a teacher, a diplomat or a nurse. If not overtly, such a person will certainly be involved in helping others in some way, even if on a voluntary basis and in some kind of charity... or two... or three! It might be somebody spending a lot of time organizing jumble sales, baking cakes for school fairs etc. It's a person who has a very practical intelligence which is circled around the needs of others.

She might be fleshy and strongly built yet her feet and hands seem small. She has solid hips and thighs; her feet are either firmly on the ground –or if in an unbalanced state, she might have difficulties putting her feet on the ground. Her heaviness does not stop her from being quick and efficient, accomplishing her tasks with gusto. She is a patient listener who makes people comfortable, but does not hide her own feelings either. She is protective not only towards her family, but also to an extended network of friends. She thrives when needed by others, to the extent of forgetting her own needs, which might leave her feeling empty and unfulfilled. She mistakes this emptiness for hunger, craves for food and eating becomes a "must". Eating despite being "full" slows her metabolism; food remains undigested, inflating her abdomen with stagnant energy, fluid and gas. As the body can't make use of the food, she feels "low" and her remedy is to eat more. This leads to extra physical weight making her sluggish, tired and feeling "stuck". **This "being stuck"** expresses at the psychological level as holding on; holding on to ideas and opinions with unrivalled stubbornness.

If the environment is generous, without too much change and with lots of social tasks to fulfil she will be happy and have a stabilising effect on the world around her. Her life is like a play: she supports the players, providing physical and mental nourishment, thus ensuring that the play of the world can continue and that every other player can do their part.

She radiates love, sympathy and compassion which arise from **understanding that we are all children of ONE EARTH!**

From that comes the recognition that you are my brother, my sister, that there is only one brother/sisterhood of man. Being aware of that enables her to recognise the physical, material and psychological suffering of others; I can "step into your shoes". This centrally orientated empathy rises from a core-awareness of the belly; it's "felt in the guts".

Imbalances in the Earth Element might eventually result in benevolent lumps of one sort and another in the tissues, since "disease (for Earth-people) is located within the flesh". And since the Earth Element covers feeding others, her mammary glands might especially be affected. She is also prone to fibroids, especially in the womb.

People, with a dominant Earth–energy might walk with a slight inward shuffle, such as can be observed in old people. This is described as "an apraxia of gait" which is characterised as a slow, halting, short-stepped, shuffling or sliding gait." In fact, the feet might be dragged, as though "sticking to the earth", or people might appear as though on their tiptoes, cut off from the earth. By contrast, in a person with strong balanced earth energy, focus comes from the centre, their belly. They stand poised strong and stable.

So how to balance the earth energy? The Tibetan Buddhist Healer and Teacher, venerable T.Y.S. Lama Gangchen explains that "we have caused overwhelming outer and inner pollution, the decline and misuse of natural resources… resulting in… violent crime, drug abuse and ever increasing body and mind sickness... we all possess a precious human body; if we use it negatively, we can contribute to our personal and planetary suicide. We can choose to go from darkness to darkness, from light to darkness or from darkness to light or from light to light. The choice is ours." (Ngal-So; p.153)

Whether in the environment, in general or within our own Being, the first step to heal our Earth is to find out who you are, what your needs are; then find what you can do to ensure that you fulfil your potential? In nature, Earth needs to be ploughed over, dug up, opened up - to let the air in; it needs to be watered to provide moisture for growth; it needs seeds that fulfil the need to create many abundant forms; it needs the sun to warm the earth. In other words **Earth needs to work in conjunction with the other Elements. So** what do you need from Mother Earth? A mudpack or someone to defend your rights?

The Earth-goddess has many faces, from life giving mother to giver of learning and wisdom, to upholder of the laws and their defender, as warrior and destroyer. I have a friend, who whenever she feels down, simply lays, spread-eagle fashion on the ground. Others recommend walking barefoot on grass, beach, even stones. Another simple way of getting in touch with earth and replenishing your earth energy is gardening; get out of your head... into your garden!

Again, whether in the environment or in our body, w**hen the Earth Element itself is ill, then all else will be affected; after all She is the hub, the Centre...**This is the peril of our time; serious disruption of the energy flow is at stake.

However **to heal the earth, within an earth person a sensible diet is adamant**. The quality of food in our times is generally low; it is mass produced (artificial ripening, long transportation, refrigeration etc.), with loads of chemicals (fertilizers, insecticides, herbicides etc.), then often processed (irradiation, freezing, additives excess use of oils and sugar etc.) and consumed with little care and attention. On top of that, these days we are confronted with genetically engineering food which adds all sorts of genes (i.e. fish and pig genes are now added to tomatoes!) So it is almost impossible to get good food. Right food that is medicine for the Earth- energy, are Yam, pumpkins, potatoes, carrots, turnips, millet and rice; late summer fruit such as apricots, pears etc. Minerals are very important for the Earth, (they are earth!). How important these are, I experienced one year in India. I stayed for a prolonged time in an ashram and as advised, I drank a lot of water, as the heat of the day made me sweat a lot, especially during work periods. I got weaker and weaker - the water, although in itself important, washed out important minerals. Eventually an Ayurvedic doctor suggested adding ionized minerals to the water; I drank the ionized water - in 24 hours I was fine! Of course the traditional ways of Shiatsu, Acupuncture, Zero Balancing etc. are helpful, but for the earth person massages are especially recommended.

If earth-energy is out of balance on the subtle level, a different solution might be needed: The North American Indian tradition has a way that combines several levels. They suggest we go on a "vision quest" to a power place. Under the guidance of a Medicine Person the seeker is to find a location, where the aspirant feels the power of the earth; there he fasts and prays for three or four days. Some people walk a long time to find such a place - some walk literally (or metaphorically) a lifetime. Jesus went to the desert or to the sea, Buddha went to the Bodhi Tree, Abraham went into the wilderness, and Merlin went into the crystal cave in Wales (UK). Once we have found our place of power "the attention of Mother Earth is directed to that spot, and energy begins to flow to that area, the Earth Mother is there to nurture and give solace to that person, a vision, a direction or healing". The key is trusting and being silent. This, in essence is meditation!

But maybe you need to change your job! Hands are used therapeutically in jobs such as a potter, practicing crafts like papier-mâché, weaving and spinning; simple, everyday things like cooking are not surprisingly connected to the Earth Element. This might mean you have to change your lifestyle – YES! "Isn't there some medicine I can take?" - Nothing happens without the will to change; that is an Earth problem in itself; once they have lost their core-energy, they rather hand over to others. Healing your Earth is to reconnect with your centre; and remember you are not living alone we are all earth's children!

How does a person with dominant Earth energy interact and react to people characterized by other Elements, i.e. **Earth and Water!** Earth's stability and solidity is contrasted by water's fluidity. Earth is dense and stable; water is transparent and adaptable/fluid. However they complement each other, water gives moisture and enables the earth to be fertile; earth gives water the badly needed stability. Myths in all cultures testify to this archetypal fertile relationship; i.e. Earth, the female goddess is fertilized by water in the form of the rain–god. (After all from their union the first life microbes and amoebas arose). The deep connection between these two shows in the landscape. Earth banks channel the river's water to its destiny, the ocean.

The ocean bottom, however deep, is still earth! Islands scattered in the oceans, show how much the earth can penetrate into the kingdom of Water. A relationship between people characterised by Earth and Water is peaceful and fertile as long as they respect each other's boundaries; the stability of the one must be balanced by the flexibility of the other. They can be creative and inspired, supporting each other's duties, jobs and ambitions. As we saw above, danger comes if either one dominates; the Earth person can be made ineffective, lethargic and drown if Water is too strong; Earth gets swamped and loses its ability to hold. The key word here is: discipline. If the Earth person resists the temptation to "close ranks" and become a stubborn, inflexible rock and Water disciplines its drive to "go all over the place", and instead accepts the guiding river banks of the Earth person, then a balanced and unusual fertile relationship can grow.

Next, let's look at the relationship between Earth and Fire. Imagine a bonfire; watch what goes on between the earth on which the fire sits and the fire itself. Earth herself does not get consumed by fire; the next day, we find a heap of ashes (minerals) on the earth; after the next rainfall even those have even been assimilated by earth. The Chinese talk of the Earth as the daughter of the Fire. Cosmologically, this is certainly true: over millions of years a fiery star became – our earth. The same process still goes on as the core of the earth cools. Occasionally we witness fire breaking out from within the earth and producing lava, which in turn, cooled and eroded, is again earth. Fire whether inside the earth and outside adds to earth. What does this mean in terms of relationships between an Earth – and a Fire-person?

From the perspective of the earth-person fire warms, comforts it, inspires it to such an extent that ultimately the Earth person might be melted by a passion that changes her own being to light. Enthusiasm and joy are infused in the otherwise heavy and dense Earth person, so that her innate glow of love and concern for others can "brighten up the world". If she finds the fire of devotion and love, her work might expand to great humanitarian work. She might become a light for others in her own right. But if for one reason or the other the Fire is removed, the Earth person, left to herself cannot maintain the warm lightness for long, and returns to her more heavy and dense states. She needs Fire; so ultimately she needs to discover her own source of Fire, which might be an inspiring job, charitable or humanitarian causes - or finding a spiritual teacher so she can discover her own divinity.

Earth and Air seem so different! Earth appears as solid matter- and Air is so light, so insubstantial; they seem opposite. Air is rarely still; it drifts here and there over the surface of the earth. Rarely is there any interaction between the two, except may be in violent storms. Each keeps in their realm. Other agents like microbes and fungus are needed to bring air to penetrate into the earth. Earth is surrounded by Air, it almost "suffocates" it; this band of air is subtle but never the less substantial, it is some 4oo km deep gradually thinning. However strong the centre of earth, it cannot hold the gases of the air eternally.

Without enriching organisms, the elemental relationship of Air, Earth is life-less, at best peaceful, an uneventful coexistence – at worst stale. There would be little conflict between the two but a respectful coexistence. The Earth person being by nature supportive and able to serve with dignity, respects the Air persons and holds them as close as possible, with understanding and respect. Yet the Air person can't help "thinning-out", this self-removal of the Air person does not have to be intentional, but can simply be a business-project far away, or Air's tendency to shut others out. ("gone fishing!"- literally or mentally retreating "into the garden shed".) True interaction between them - from the point of the Earth - can only be through a catalyst (children?).

The relationship between **Earth and the fifth Element** (in Chinese tradition named Wood; in others ether or Spirit, or faith etc. having strong "spiritual overtones.") The Fifth Element refers to That which contains everything even time and causation. Earth is the densest, most manifest amongst the elements, Space the least "substantial"; it seems to have no "real" perceivable substance, hence the Space person might seem detached from the humdrum of life; one can't "nail her down"; she may be simply disinterested or have her mind filled with a plethora of ideas, that she can't make “real”. As for relating between an Earth- and a Space person, it appears as though they have even less in common than Earth and Air, but not so. Space is in every particle of Earth, down to the subatomic level. And… earth after all exists totally within Space; there is mutual integration. Earth knows that it is totally held and interpenetrated by Space. Space knows her every niche and crevice. A weak earth can be “sucked into a black hole”. On the other hand if the Earth person has enough strength (gravity) from her centre, it “hangs” rather autonomously in Space; the Earth person can lead a fulfilling, autonomous life within the Space person’s orbit.

Being opposites, they are mutually complementing, giving each other meaning of life; this is an avenue a couple could explore. Earth’s centre is her own strength (gravity); Space lives in an altogether different dimension. For the Earth person, a quantum leap is required to get into touch with That.

If Earth focuses within, Space focuses beyond. For such a relationship to work, awareness is more important than ever; and that starts with earth’s awareness of her own centre: “Who am I”?

Water, its season and relationships.

In Northern Europe, the trees start looking bare in November, all the leaves drop from trees; and it gets increasingly cold. Living in a densely wooded valley, this has its advantages. I can see the other side of the valley; the sky is bigger! What joy! Winter is starting. It never stops amazing me, how even when I go to New Zealand, in the middle of European summer …there is winter.

Winter is not a date on the calendar but a quality of energy. It's a shift to a different mode of existence, no matter where one is. **The season we call "Winter" is related to the Element 'Water'**. Winter is when all energies, be it the sap in the trees, or the life-force in us, has drawn inwards, resting in preparation for new growth. It's this aspect which we associated with the energy-field we call 'Water'. Contemplate: after water has done its job of nurturing and purifying, after completing one of its 'life-cycles', it sinks deep into the bowels of the earth. There it rests, from there, stripped of pollutants water rises as the freshest "spring" to new life.

Even those countries which experience not the classical symptoms of winter, however, partake in similar energies. In Monsoon times for example, enormous quantities of water sink deep into the bowels of the earth, to rest after the great storms.

In some parts of the world, water stays on the surface (without going deep) – and rests, it crystallizes becoming ice, a frozen river or glacier. Picture the arctic continent or the eternal snow on mountain ranges like the Himalayas or Andes and realize the inherent power in this quiet state of 'reflection'.

In deep rest, such frozen water retains the memory of its

experiences (Masaru Emoto; 'The hidden message of water') and once rested, it thaws ready for a new adventure. The melted water still has some of the memory, some of the knowledge from before; however it is re- newed, "re-born".

Be it the stillness of a winter's day, the snow flake or a lake of ice, - or even the deep reservoirs of ground water in the tropics, all are just grades of manifestation of this deep rest. It is **frequently associated with the stillness we call death.** Yet death, just like the temporary state of winter is a transitory state; now water is ice, now it flows; now it evaporates, the vessel having been emptied, soon it will be replaced and filled with new energy, new growth. Especially old people are frightened by the thought of this transition. Partly because of a tendency to ponder an 'unfulfilled, painful life'; they attach themselves to the autumn, the past, the memories and then they stay left alone, isolating themselves in hopelessness or try to escape their thoughts by constant distraction. To prepare for the 'winter of one's life' and death is so frightening to some, that they need endless rounds of meaningless socialising, bingo, games etc.

Even young people sometimes fall prey to the same imbalance. They too need 'winter' to contemplate what is happening in their life. But all too often they drown themselves in endless rounds of parties, deafening music, even drugs – these are signs of imbalances in the flow of 'Water' energy. Such imbalances are easily recognisable, because people (young or old) positively dislike winter. Aloneness and introversion frighten them. (This is vastly different from the seclusion of a contemplative who despite apparently withdrawing, stays alert and connected albeit on a subtle level.) We can observe such imbalance in the Water Element even in our society at large. Constant distraction, constant stimulus…keep the society stressed and busy- no time to rest and reflect…as a result, **we as a society, cause “Water” imbalances on a massive scale on the body of our planet earth.** For example:

- Glacial ice is melting, (Montana’s National Glacier Park, created 1910 used to have 150 glaciers…now there are 30)
- Polar ice is melting in the Arctic and Patagonia (Glaciers and Ice-sheets in the latter have disappeared…exposing bare rock)
- Ice caps are said to have shrunk by 9 %. (In the Antarctic Region, Ice sheets the size of California have melted in 2005).

We hear or see these statistics, but only if one flies over the arctic sea can one see the actual impact; and yes the damage is not limited to the effect of melting ice. The cold of emotional winter also is very damaging. Ice is not just a beautiful storehouse of future energy, it has inherent danger. Flowing water nurtures, frozen water kills! Furthermore, ice-sheets are cuttingly sharp, (eating i.e. at coastal landscapes) and ice-spikes used wrongly, can be lethal weapons - just like a knife. Furthermore ice is brittle and breaks. Where isolation has created such sheets of dry ice, such ‘brittle-ness,’ in a person, there is danger of becoming manic or insane, people who completely withdraw into a calcified state of themselves, pondering on nothing but the past, fate and isolation become depressed; a dangerous Water –imbalance.

Everything has many aspects; the most beautiful images of winter are connected to the northern hemisphere. There are snow-scapes of immense pure beauty and harmony, radiating great peace.

There is especially beautiful clear light in the north; and who hasn't seen the aurora borealis (at least on a photo), a well-known occurrence of special light. Standing at the most northern point of Europe, the North Cape (Honigsveg, Norway) the majestic stillness is palatable, there is a feeling of limitless expansion; watching what seems like shimmering light reflected in light - is unforgettable. In many indigenous traditions, the north is the place of the elders, those wisdom keepers who hold ancient knowledge.

And yet the north, as winter - is also associated with darkness, long nights, dark feelings, long suffering, dark emotions and the fear of the unknown. Many people are afraid of the waters, the ocean - because it evokes this feeling in them. However in the stillness of our very being, we experience both sides of life, the special light of consciousness and the darkness of material existence and realise: they are One.

Winter and the long nights of the north have another interesting resonance with the cycle of water. We might prefer sunshine, we might wish for lighter days…just as we might wish for rain… but the cycle needs to run its course; we cannot change it. We simply need to learn to trust that one day spring will come, one day light will rise, one day it will rain again, that day will break again and …one day suffering will change to joy! One of "Water's" gifts **is to learn to trust.** The fruit of trust is **a healthy detachment:** one doesn't get bogged down by details and circumstances, but knows all will change! With trust and detachment "Water" invites us to simply 'Be.' **Being is total integrity with who you are; at any time water is totally itself yet totally willing to change in ever new forms.**

Problems arise when we are unwilling to change, when people are frozen in their position, their attitudes, their opinions – or their relationship to their own physical existence. From those imbalances in the Water Element many illnesses are created (whether they stem from mental or physical "being cold"). Many arthritic problems are, for example, made a lot worse in cold weather - pains increase, joints stiffen. But when we speak of a 'cold person,' we are not thinking of their body temperature, we are thinking of people who are unable or unwilling to express human warmth. A mother who lacks the ability to hug, touch, warm and cuddle her child has an imbalance in "Water."

Many people in our society live a stressful, self-orientated life, taking no time to care much about the suffering of others. Their stress aggravates their kidneys and adrenals and stops them from caring. Again it highlights the Water imbalance, in our society, and this imbalance creates fear (the opposite of the balanced state of

"Water" which shows trust and its result fearlessness). Imbalanced "Water" (be it in a person or a society) creates fear. Modern societies as a whole are frequently ruled by fear; fear of attack, fear of not having enough, fear of economic crashes (so we create one-just to feel justified) fear of not being accepted by others, etc.etc. The connection of Water energy to kidneys (including the endocrine glands with their flight or fight response) makes this obvious.

In the cycle of its life, water constantly changes its form, implying there is constantly danger of losing the sense of self, one's personal boundaries; the ego reacts by *holding on to what was!* It constantly opposes change – this poisons the nature of water. Fear is like a paralysed sphincter that cannot let go of the urine and the vessel is not emptied. The illusion is that by holding onto the old, nothing new can come in, but by necessity it does! The river of life flows on regardless; in the extreme, fear becomes panic, one suffocates into despair, deep depression, even paranoia.

How to balance such tendencies? To see that the nature of water is to flow, the nature of life is change. Change is inherent in all life; hence we need to practice love and respect of all existence at any moment. The principal behind that is ***Ahimsa. Ahimsa* is the dharma of Water,** the supreme *dharma;* **he who practices *Ahimsa* leads a life of freedom from fear.** When totally established in non-harming the peaceful vibes are so strong, that even lions, snakes or other wild animals lie down at one's feet.' O. M. Aivanhov a Bulgarian Sage, pulls water and Ahimsa together, stating that: water deserves our respect because it is part of every living and non-living being. Giving respect to all is practicing *ahimsa.* It starts with treating your child with respect for it is a unique life form with unique needs and not 'just a kid' (kid being an American slang word for a child)! It includes listening to people for that is a mark of respect to the unique life form that speaks to you. It refers to giving people the right jobs and adequate pay for their job, because otherwise it violates human dignity. It even relates to how we build our houses and cities, how we manage our business; or small things in daily life, such as not having the radio on too loud – not venting our anger at each other! It relates to the way we drive our car with politeness rather than pushing others off the road; it relates to the tone of voice we communicate in, and it even relates to the way we look at each other. The principle of Non- harming in the final analysis is **service to others, just like water serves all Beings.**

So to balance the Water Energy, in our own life as much as in society and our relationships with each-other we need to cultivate Ahimsa. But what else can we do, especially **to balance the Water Element in our own being? T**here are two pointers: 1) maintaining an even, steady flow of energy, and using one's available energy appropriately measured; and 2) ensuring the purity of energy; for that, we need to ensure an intake of right food; i.e. when the kidneys become blocked from fats, salt, cholesterol and stress, the amount of *Qi* that reaches the organs and lower back is diminished.

Water has been recognized as a healing agent for thousands of years in all traditions, most of us will have experienced saunas, being sprayed or sluiced by water jets (many homes nowadays have Jacuzzis), or under-water-massage, be it by bubbles or human hands. Hardly anybody takes a bath anymore without adding aromatherapy oils of one kind of another; or simply sea-salt. This goes back to quite a tradition. Priessnitz, Dr Kneipp or Dr Gully et all, build their therapies on the belief that water is capable of curing every disease 'by dissolving the diseased matter and enabling it to be expelled from the body.'

I remember as an asthmatic child being taken to the special healing places, where salt water was run down walls built of twigs, about five meters high. The air was saturated with fine spray to be inhaled; we walked slowly and with measured steps and expanded chest for deep breathing around such 'Salinen', or sat - wrapped in blankets, within feet of the dripping water and read. This process has the same nourishing effect for kidneys and lungs as living near the sea. Today even Baths that recreate the amniotic fluid are available, and of course swimming, gentle exercise or relaxation in pools or the sea, or in hot sulphur springs are all common therapeutic ways of balancing today.

Other less 'watery' ways can be used to help the Water Energy of the body. As with the other elements, traditional ways of complementary medicine such as Acupuncture, Shiatsu, Massage etc. can be successfully used. To increase the flow and soften the character of Water Energy listening to music, dance and art therapy and all manner of slow exercises such as Tai Chi and slow Hatha Yoga can be recommended. Exercises that stretch the back of the trunk and legs are especially to be recommended. But equally and less straining is just sitting by a waterfall, listening and/or contemplating a still pond or a clear lake, listening to the sound of falling rain. Tuning into the lashing waves on a beach also helps to balance "Water"; it flushes out and dilutes the impurities of the emotional body.

Frequently people are reminded of drinking a lot of water, to drink too much liquid though, overworks the kidneys and then they tend to tire easily. A person with swollen areas below the eyes is showing such fatigue; the kidneys cannot cope with the amount of water. It is even worse if the person drinks a lot of toxins and stimulants, such as alcohol or tea and coffee, which tend to colour the 'bags under the eyes' into dark rings; increasing dark areas signal severe problems with the Water- Energy, i.e. illness. It would be good to eat a diet that does not put so many impurities in the body (that they need flushing out) so that the kidneys do not have to work so hard!

What then would be good to eat for a person with the main characteristics of "Water"? Foods are chosen here for their ability to enhance the functioning of the kidneys, such as beans and salty foods (small amounts stimulate their work); barley and buckwheat in terms of grain; all sea vegetables support the kidneys. Foods are also chosen for supplementing and regulating moisture. Illness caused by the Water Element is often connected to cold – thus warming food is essential to support the kidneys, such as ginger root (as spice, tea or vegetable), garlic, chilli, mustard seeds, coriander and cardamom seeds. Kidney energy is a limited resource, so to replenish its essence, dioscorea root is recommended, as are rehmannia root, black fungus and other mushrooms and the cornus fruit, all found in Chinese herbal shops.

If we mistreat our body (himsa / harmfull action) by eating the wrong diet (too many refined foods carrying chemical toxins, fat, cholesterol, too many salts etc.) or use too much of that energy by leading a harmful lifestyle (excessive sex, too much stress, continued fear and excitement/shock), it will suffer! A dangerous lifestyle, abortions, misuse of drugs or abuse of our bodies in any way, will irreversibly deplete the Water Energy and an untimely death will follow.

The body is the servant of our spiritual growth, through the body alone the soul can learn in this school of life, through the body alone we have the ability to evolve, to grow towards greater understanding, to higher wisdom. Thus it is important to keep the Water Energy in a steady and even flow; in fact it is said that the origin of Yoga is to prolong the body's life to fulfil our spiritual purpose. Understanding and protecting the body are acts of spiritual mastery.

However we live not alone. We said previously, that each person is manifesting a mixture of the five Elemental energies with one energy dominant.

So how does a Water-person relate to other people? They have the ability to nurture and heal others , as well as being adaptable to fit into various circumstances of life, with ease...but amongst all he/she serves. In order to be able to do that, the person also needs rest and solitude to regenerate and renew. Of course there is more, but let's just stick with that.

How would such a person relate to another, say a partner, a wife, a boss or a friend dominantly characterised by the **Earth Element.** To understand their relationship, let's contemplate some aspects from the perspective of water. Entering the cycle of life for water, where rain touches the ground- at first it seeps into earth, water feels welcome and wanted. Water loves to explore this apparently solid element, sinking into every niche and aspect. How different it is!

"Earth" becomes the support and vessel that water needs in order to travel to the place where it is needed. However eventually water sinks into depths were it will join more water (meeting like-minded people - a drop of water by itself 'dries -up' quickly.) Meaning: The Water-person enjoys the relationship with earth- they complement each other fulfilling each other's needs for creativity. But ultimately "Water" might "sink deeper" withdraw and seek the company of like-minded. If the earth person allows this to happen, the relationship is probably the most stable and fruitful, with mutual support and trust. When there is conflict, even when fear and anger surface, the Water-person withdraws, pauses (may be only for minutes) then from reaching the stillness within him/herself reaches out in concern for the other.

What about the relationship of "Water" with Fire-people? Imagine a bowl of water on your windowsill, the sun shining on it gradually warms the water; then put the same bowl into the freezer, water turns to ice. From the perspective of water, it looks as though in order to fulfil its destiny of flowing and nurturing, water cannot be without its 'arch-enemy.'

Yet what happens when water gets 'too warm'? It changes into vapour and rises. As steam, water can achieve great feats, i.e. driving turbines, moving railway engines, at worst even as a hydrogen bomb, such great power comes from the combined force of water and fire!

And yet, the bowl of water left on the windowsill for too long (exposed to the sun) will soon have no water left in it. The water has not only changed its shape (vapour) but it has evaporated; to all intents and purpose it escaped into the atmosphere in order to reconvene with other moisture and gather as a cloud filled with water. (Note: whether sinking into earth (manifest) or ascending to Space- "Water" seeks like-minded company!) Fire might appear to destroy water, but it merely speeds up its life cycle. With the help of fire, water runs through the cycles of its existence faster and often more efficiently, albeit not less traumatically.

There are many other aspects to contemplate, such as:
-The appropriate warmth fire gives to water has great effects; think how the gulf-stream influences climates.
- Appropriate use of warm water has great healing effects in all manner of medicines.
- Water reflects light! Etc. etc.

Summing up: although water is threatened by fire, it **is dependent on Fire for its fulfilment of purpose (ice cannot flow)** Of course, this fire does not need to come from another person, but can come from within the same person, as we are all Elements, at any time.

In the relationship between a Water and a Fire-person it is important to realize that they need each other – yet their extremes threaten the existence of the partner.

Water-people get drained, overruled and exhausted if the Fire-person is too active, loud, demanding, aggressive, too volatile and flamboyant. For a while "Water" tries, due to its adaptability, to accommodate such temperament; it will change its own shape to reach giddy heights- but in the long term it puts too great demands on "Water". Most Water- people would not dream of getting involved in such high voltage Fire - they would intuit that such a relationship could explode and destroy either or both. Being aware in their depth of this potential danger, it might fill the Water-person with fear. Water's inherent willingness to adapt might have to be curbed purely for self-preservation, choosing to withdraw, to be warmed from a distance, only. However if the people involved are aware and balanced in themselves, they might rise together and achieve great feats; they could trigger colossal changes in people and societies.

How do Water and Air relate? For most parts on the surface of the globe, water is covered by air; air sits on top seemingly doing its own thing! But on a closer look, air causes ripples and waves, waves that affect the water so deeply that they determine the currents and flow of oceans and at times cause huge upheavals in giant storm waves. Water also is penetrated by Air (oxygen) which causes bubbles (ideas) occasionally this interaction gets so entangled and mixed up, that they foam and froth together. Water is moved by Air, motivated to go where it needs to; even pushing it hard, yet without the danger that fire poses.

In a partnership or relation between two such people, Air is the active partner; water simply accepts air's pushing. However water has huge determination and when its power is released it is a match for Air. Just watch the passionate, angry reactions where water and air "thrash it out in magnificent storms!" This 'thrashing' can be driven by passion; the high waves of fun however don't last. In the main, such struggle ends with either temporary or final separation of the two, when they each withdraw into their own energy fields to recuperate. Neither of them though, can fully follow the other; water withdraws into depth, air ascends to heights.

No doubt there are many more aspects between these two elements that can be contemplated, for example: both share an important chemical: oxygen, both are renowned for their clarity and cleanliness; both have the ability to analyse and penetrate deeply intellectually, being creative thinkers. Yet they use their abilities differently. Air cuts away sharply and thus indulges intellectually, "Water" is more reflective, mirrors the wholeness of life.

As long as both contribute their angle, they benefit from each other and help others with their wisdom, **one leans on Bhakti Yoga, the other on Jnana Yoga**. When these two combine great service can be rendered. A pattern of efficient interaction can be created between the two, in order to serve where needed; they both are main carriers of prana, of life-sustaining energy, of life-force!

Finally we come to the relationship of **Water and Space**. If we look at space as outer space - there is simply no interaction! However in a worldly sphere, whatever water does, occupies space; water completes its whole life-cycle within space! What appears as no interaction is - from the point of view of water - total involvement. It could be a one-sided relationship.

However in a marriage or in general interactions, these two can have much understanding and much to share, in the normal world of relativity. If Space can be content with limiting itself and not be distracted from the relationship, it is hugely beneficial for "Water" – it helps "Water" to achieve his dharma fully. Yet however close the couple appears to be, they can easily be pulled apart by the extra needs of the Space Element which 'leaves water behind.' When for example the Space-person gets involved into something/someone else, the wound it leaves in the Water-person is substantial; he/she literally sinks into the depths of despair. On the other hand, the sensitivity of "Water" might alert him/her and relax into 'understanding'.

As water flows through all of us, so does divine energy, which encourages "Water" to make highly moral decisions, from an awareness of the unity between all Beings. How can I hurt somebody that feels just like me? It makes no sense, it means I hurt or hate myself. This empathy of "Water" is its greatest message reaching far beyond the physical, psychic or social realm. How can we slaughter an animal, cut a tree or poison a well when all of creation shares the same energy in just a different shape. Understanding this, "Water" is able to relate with relative ease to all of the five psychological Element Types.

Fire, its season and relationships.

Normally one would rightly associate the energy-field we call Fire, with summer for the obvious reason it is the time of great vitality, of generous growth and abundance. Similarly in human terms, the years of family life and career are associated with it; we talk of the summer of life, with its warmth of family life, its abundance and ripening of ideas, achievements and direction in life.

However that is looking at Fire burning bright, looking at its furthest expansion, i.e. it brightest manifestation. On the other end of the scale, that brightness starts somewhere, it starts in mid-winter.

In the darkest part of the year there is a turning point. At the winter solstice, energy changes, light rises and starts to expand. Indigenous cultures and 'people of old' used to pay great homage to this 'rising light'. The fact that we celebrate Christmas at this particular time of the calendar is not because Jesus, the Carpenter's son was born then (we don't really know when that was) but His existence brought light into the world. He became the Christ, a "Shining One", an Illumined Being. To celebrate this, the 'people of old' choose the winter- solstice, the time of rising light.

I lived at the most Western edge of Europe, and in the Mythology of these lands, the sun plays a hugely important part. Here, in the West, the sun disappears for its underground journey of revival and rebirth. It is said that here, the 'Otherworld' and the relative world meet, the doors to the 'Otherworld' are open, so that there is no real division between the two. **At the winter solstice the Otherworld (not underworld!) awakes, from here light rises,** beginning a new dawn, a new age, a new year begin. This 'turning-point' is the moment of quickening, of awakening, of light returning. This is still celebrated today. People of all ages assemble on the hill-tops at sun-rise on the day of the solstice and watch the ascending light being born; and they chant… and may be you will not believe me, but I have witnessed them chant the Gayatri (it might be a new Age influence, but…).

So the winter solstice signifies that moment when Fire-energy is ignited, resuming its cyclic movement. This tiny spark of **Awakening**. Celtic Shamanic ceremonies celebrate this awakening as the moment we become aware of something beyond the material world, from then on we walk the path! We begin to understand and begin to put forth effort (tapasya).

What is it we understand? Matter is inherently light; it goes permanently through a process of transforming itself to become light. Fire needs something to burn, and the result of matter burning - is light. This transformation is not a miracle because fire/light is inherent in all matter. Just cast your mind back to the beginning of the beginning: solar winds swirled and coagulated into a ball which cooled to be this world, eventually unfolding as you and me. Light is our origin and destiny. The process of this change we call "burning". Fire- energy is both the manifesting and dissolving agent of this process.

Now let's look one step further. This light that we celebrate is what? We can - but here is not the place - to argue the case that light is consciousness. It carries knowing (con-science). There are many religious traditions that equal consciousness, light and God. Fire then becomes a symbol - or a manifestation of "God". No wonder most cultures have as their central deity a version of a Fire-God (Agni) Sun-God (Surya) or Goddess (Savitri). With Fire we open the door to the subtler realms of understanding, of wisdom; we allow the fire to burn us, i.e. to "transform base-metal…to gold". If we allow ourselves to learn from the experiences of our lives – we are transformed by the "fire of knowledge" to eventually return to our original nature (Patanjali) to become pure light, pure consciousness. Fully awakened to That. **Buddhi becomes Buddha, an Awakened One**

The process starts somewhere, it starts in the darkest night, the mystics talk of the dark night of the soul. So when we celebrate the rising of light in December; we celebrate our original nature, our birthday…not just Jesus Christ's birthday. With it we awaken anew to the awareness of being light.

When we begin to open ourselves to this re-turn journey, we open ourselves to working with the Fire-energy. Hence **Yoga is described by Swami Rama of the Himalayas as the path of 'Fire and Light'!** If we do not learn from our experience, if we stay in the darkness of ignorance we choose the cold, the dark, the suffering.

One particular illness that befalls people who are dominated by the energy-field of 'Fire' is especially that, they become depressed, or they get angry and frustrated that the material world does not give them what they want! Fire needs constant "food" to burn. The material world needs to give me; I want – whatever they reap, successes or failures is not enough; because they do not learn from their experience. So they demand louder, drive themselves harder to material gain and success - hoping that it will ease their Being. But remaining in the material realm they cannot "see" the place where material world and the "Otherworld" meet, and all is given. They drive themselves blindly and burn out, becoming ashes from which no more light can emanate.

Of course here we have only looked at the tiniest aspect of the element Fire. However that aspect of **not being able to learn from our experience (for whatever reason), of not being able to see the 'rising light' but remaining in darkness of ignorance, is an enormous source of suffering**. With it or from it, all manner of 'dis-ease' and imbalances are created, just as from the opposite extreme of excessive burning – both poles of the same energy create similar symptoms. In both cases the question arises how can we find the mid-line, the point of balance. Where **Fire Energy** warms, inspires, illuminates and gives light without blinding, is steady and tranquil without feeling bored, is responsive to what life gives without hunting after each opportunity. How can we entice Fire Energy to be its best: joyful, happy, content and celebrating life? William Wordsworth described the state beautifully:

> With an eye made quiet by the power of harmony,
> and the deep power of joy, see into the life of things.

There are as always the outside agents that can help, such as Acupuncturists, Shiatsu practitioners and all manner of therapists and energy workers, who might help us to re-educate our body energy, but we can do a lot ourselves. Gentle, cooling forms of Yogic exercises, as well as Makkaho exercises (Masunaga and Ohashi). Practicing Tai Chi has been recommended by cardiologists for patients who have or are threatened with heart disease; palpitations, angina or hypertension. Another **home remedy worth mentioning** might be that of rubbing your skin vigorously in the morning when you have your bath or shower, with a brush or hard sponge (*loofa*). Hot and cold alternative showers are good for low Fire-energies, and cooling water therapies, including swimming are good for high Fire-energies. A person with a fiery temperament is well advised to have cooling drinks, eat cooling food and live in an appropriate climate and learn such calming techniques as meditation, Yoga Nidra and some guided pranayama). To aim for a stable home-life is very good for 'grounding' Fire Energy. High flying Fire-energy needs to contemplate how to remove the source of stress (especially when the heart and other organs related to the Fire Element are threatened. Switching to a different job might help; as might a different place to live, a different relationship to others or even to oneself. Self-hypnosis, Autogenics, Autosuggestion, Yoga, walking, painting, music, sports or swimming, anything that relaxes helps.

As we know, **diet plays a major role** in heart disease; i.e. the consumption of cholesterol, fatty foods, meats etc. are high risk factors and are often accompanied by a low intake of dietary fibre. A Nutritionist or herbalist should be consulted for more specific advice. However we met the two extremes of Fire-energy…. Too much and too little! Both need help. High Fire- energy needs cold food like salads and fresh fruit, whereas low Fire- energy needs stimulating through gentle spices and cooked, warming food, such as porridge, soups and stews.

And there is one special remedy: **The Fire person needs to discover its own heart**, it needs to learn to listen to the quietness of their heart, from there the vital love of self emanates; Fire-people crave love, where better to find it than in their own heart, and then love can flow to all others. It must be the most stunning revelation that love is not given to us from anybody; not from you, not from a husband or child, not from any agent outside ourselves. This love is in us! It is the nature of pure life energy, it is us; it flows through us, for us, to nourish us, to warm us and from us to give to others. We are the source of the love we need and the instrument of the love we give. Indian philosophy has it, that we are characterised by three qualities: Sat (existence) chid (consciousness) ananda (bliss, joy). We exist, we are aware, and we are joy. Not bad! Meditate on that! That is to awake to the light you are!

And do not forget that you are surrounded by light! We do not live alone, but life itself is being "in relationship". **A Fire- person if in balance, will be especially warm to others, amusing and inspiring to her peers and the community, provide a happy home and entertainment for her many friends.** She would be a person with seemingly limitless energy that leads an active life; her intimate relationship would be characterised by warmth and passion. However as we know Fire people oscillate, between burning bright and nearly being ashes, so in relationships they tend to be rather unstable and once a friend, lover or partner is familiar, they might experience a lack of stimulus. The Fire-person then leaves and goes to search elsewhere; hopefully in a book, or a hobby, but quiet likely in an endless chain of love - affairs.

This behaviour pattern can be broken if they learn to **find the love and stimulus they look for in themselves,** in their own imaginative and extremely creative personality. If not they tend to look to chocolate, coffee, alcohol or even drugs in order to maintain the constant stimulus (something to burn) their body needs. Because they are so active, their body burns the food they provide quickly and the body runs out (burns out). This condition leads to extreme exhaustion, which over prolonged periods of careless living will eventually lead to heart disease, angina, and heart attacks.

BUT how does this play out in relationships, with partners, friends, family, bosses?

For that we need to look at how Fire-energy and Earth- energy relate to each other. Fire warms the earth from the outside by way of the sun, and from the inside by way of magma (molten earth, a mixture of fire and earth). Remember above we mentioned that fire generated planet Earth, something referred to in the Chinese Shen-cycle as Fire being the mother of earth. It still nurtures and warms it. Fire (sun-light/warms) is also the instigator of any creativity happening on earth, filling it abundantly with manifold forms. On the other hand fire (inside) is given boundaries by earth; to be freed, fire has to tear, rip, or violate the earth (volcano). This mutually limiting quality is used when dealing with forest fires; oil fires etc. and they are dammed by earth.

There is, as always, an optimal point of balance in this relationship. Then earth does not get too warm so that it can do its job without turning into useless burned out desert, and fire gives just enough to support life without running wild. From the point of fire, earth is its creation, it feels responsible for it, and maintains it, but it is also always afraid that earth might be limiting it, might stop its movement, might encroach on its space, might interfere.

Any relationship between two people with the dominant characteristics of **Fire and Earth** mirrors these. Fire has it in its nature to love; it even encourages love, warmth, lightness and joy. However, Fire might think: 'I am always the one to give and initiate actions, suggests all games and provide all stimulus!' Fire gets quickly tired of that role, 'if I don't do something, it will never happen.' When tired of the Earth-person dragging her heels, s/he will quickly look elsewhere for stimulus.

Even when earth warms up, it is a long way from fire! But its stability is necessary to give a Fire-person a base from which to 'flare up,' a stage from which to perform. Earth's lack of involvement makes such a partnership difficult, yet it can be good for at its core earth, is in total union with fire. To be harmonious earth needs to dominate (like the earth crust enveloping its centre). A lasting relationship can only succeed, when the Fire-person surrenders to the Earth- person. Hard to imagine!

How do the classical antipodes of Fire and Water relate (from the perspective of Fire)?

Deep down in his own heart, Fire loves Water; it is in its nature to love and many Fire- people love swimming, having a shower, sitting by the water - or playing music with the fluidity of flowing water! They love it because subconsciously they know it's good for them. But, let's look a bit closer:

Fire illumines the dark, deep waters and makes them transparent; it also keeps them from freezing over. Fire heats water to boiling point and evaporation. On the other hand, Fire is extinguished by water! Fire's light rays get redirected, fractured by water into something most beautiful: the ray becomes a rainbow! Fire can share a mutually enriching relationship with a Water person, because it gives warmth, gives love, light and enjoyment to the other.

Fire enjoys the cool, clear wisdom the Water-person can teach, The light of fire gets reflected by the clarity of water. Fire challenges and aggravates the Water person to the point of anger and hate, where the Water person totally loses its 'cool,' and boils over. Fire is afraid of the power of the Water person, whose calmness can cause Fire to lose its vivaciousness, its zest for life. Fire gets redirected, channelled by Water to use its energy in constructive ways, ways where the inherent talent can manifestation.

The complexity of such relationship is obvious. Fire's ideas and enthusiasm can be nourished by Water's ability to unfold ideas, making them real. Fire welcomes Water's calm refreshing qualities which help it to balance and soothe the extremes. (The latter requires two people, balanced and aware of the dangers of going to 'extremes.') The Fire person rightly fears somehow getting squashed if the Water person is dominant; Fire will react with extreme outpourings like a Fire spitting dragon: aggressive, acrid and domineering, potentially exhausting itself in his constant defensiveness. If that is so, the actual positive aspects of the partnership, like sharing ideas, lightness, flexibility, joy and warmth will be lost. But if both are mature and have learned that extreme reactions are useless, then Fire might appeal to Water's clarity and wisdom and try to illuminate her. When the Fire- person 'sparkles and dances' before her, warms her and enchants her, the Water-person simply has to accept his 'light.' In a conflict, Fire will try to dominate, to burn brighter and be more - and he will be successful!

Water will have to give up or dry up!

As we proceed through the cycle of the elements, we next look at the relationship between **Fire and Air** (from the perspective of fire). Almost by definition, fire cannot exist without air. Oxygen is - at least on earth - the medium that makes ' fire into fire.' It is the catalyst without which there is no fire. This speaks of a relationship of highest dependency. All know how Air (wind) can wipe fire into frenzy and drive it to ever greater heights, be they creative or destructive.

But there is more to this relationship. Fire, as we know, has different forms. Of the three: light, warmth and flame, the burning flame is what needs oxygen; light and warmth are effects, of that process, they do not NEED Air. Whether the wind blows or not, the sunlight will reach the earth! Light needs air not so much to fuel it, as to filter it and direct it. Warmth exists in a sun warmed stone, or the thin earth crust on volcanic land; warmth is there whether wind or not, but the wind helps to distribute the warmth. So here we find that *different abilities of air serve different states (or forms) of fire.*

The relationship has always a certain amount of dependency in it, but if appearing in its tempered forms as light or warmth, air can provide additional benefits: it might set boundaries, and it distributes the heat, so it cannot build up into destruction. Air has also the potential to diffuse fire's energy by channelling it towards a goal. It is less effective than Earth or even Water, but it takes heat into a different direction. When the Fire-person becomes too powerful, too dramatic and flamboyant and over the top with emotional reactions, it might be the Air partner who, in the most natural and gentle way, can curb this destructiveness. He/she might either withhold support - or filter out the most vicious rays (or tantrums), by simple distraction. Because of the high dependency, the Fire-person will probably accept criticism from Air more easily than from anybody else - not that it will ever accept it easily! Air can help by distracting Fire with its 'own weapons'; it can move lightly, illusively and freely skipping from here to there, so that the heat is taken off; a gentle way for regulating fire's heat

So from the point of view of Fire, a partnership with Air is close, passionate and exciting, and limitations are brought gently and with love. A desirable relationship from this perspective - unless Air whips Fire into a frenzied straw fire that burns itself out in minutes and then leaves

- or, Air finds another Fire to ignite and dances somewhere else and leaves!

Fire also can be in such a frenzy that it sucks up all the Air, but it annihilates itself in the process, as was we know from the effect of the bombing of such a town as Dresden or Hamburg, (even Hiroshima), where the fire storm was so great it used all the air, suffocating the fire itself. When Fire is left by Air, only ashes remain. It is a tragic loss for Fire. Fire likes to play games with any one of the other Element personalities, it likes to dance from one relationship to another, but when Air does treat it with the same disdain, the flame goes out! The experience might be so traumatic that Fire refuses to be ignited again.

If Earth leaves Fire – Fire will bath in its abstract glory, free of restrictions.

If Water leaves Fire – Fire will sigh with relief; no more fear of annihilation

If Air leaves Fire – Fire dies, physically, mentally or spiritually, it loses its spirit.

If Space leaves Fire – Fire knows it is only temporarily, Space will be back.

Fire and Space have an intrinsic relationship. Fire can only exist in space. That goes for the big fires such as the sun, the moon and the stars - and planets; and the small fires, from the candle light to the nuclear explosion, all happen in a certain space, or even space time continuum. Space is the "mother of Fire", it can do whatever it wants, it can burn and die, can sparkle with joy or rage with anger and hate. Space is not really bothered! Space has an infinite capacity to accept these temperamental outbursts of fire. Balanced Space-people are totally tolerant people; not even fire's gift of warmth is needed by space. Space (contrary to everybody else) has enough power and energy to do without fire. This means that the favourite game of the Fire- person - that of manipulation and blackmail for the price of warmth/love - is useless towards a Space- person. From the point of the Fire-person, that makes Space almost boring, it does not lend itself to friction, to arguments, to enthusiastic challenges, space does not ignite, it loses the thrill for the Fire- person, there is nothing coming back! Imagine a thousand-ton burning meteorite - a massive ball of fire - sails through space as though nothing has happened.

In a relationship or even marriage between a person dominated by the characteristics of Fire and one characterised by the element of Space an interesting scenario unfolds. It is as though two people live side by side. Quite possibly they share the same interests, yet they are neither competing nor stimulating each other. If in this partnership, the Fire- person is well-balanced and warm, gentle and loving, the partnership can be harmonious indeed;

the Space-partner will receive the warmth and love and mirror it.

Since space holds so much - in fact the whole universe in himself; it will have plenty to stimulate Fire's insatiable appetite for excitement, fun, love and creativity. The Fire person can let off as much steam as it wants, can be as enthusiastic as it wants; the partner will not set boundaries - Space has not got the willingness to limit fire. The Space-partner will allow Fire all the flamboyant, attention seeking behaviour Fire craves and let him/her dance to exhaustion. In fact, in his vast kingdom, Space might be busy elsewhere and not even notice that Fire totally exhausts himself.

Such 'modern' freedom holds the danger that both partners might lose sight of each other, both having a 'great life,' parallel and independent. Such independence can mean, especially for Fire (always in danger of excess and running wild), that without control from outside it will experience disaster. Mind you, this might not be the end of the relationship, because Space holds Fire even in these devastating times. The Space-partner will always be there for his fiery friend and partner, in whatever role. Fire can depend on Space for support, for nourishment and for shelter. Just as with Air there is dependency here, yet the difference is that Air fuels Fire, it 'makes it burn'; Space lets it burn if it wants to. There is much less active involvement!

Having looked at these interactions between Elements and their energy-fields as expressed in people, it is obvious, that all depends on balance, or dare I say: self-discipline! How these relationships work out, depends how much we are in charge of ourselves, how much self-discipline we can master and how much respect we bring to the other. Self-discipline and respect, that to me spells **LOVE.**

Air, its season and relationships

When one lives surrounded by "almost untouched" nature, the seasons are very obvious. I went for a walk; dry leaves are covering the ground, the branches of the tall trees are becoming visible, and at night the stars sparkle through the hitherto dense canapé of leaves. There is a crisp chill in the air, it is definitely getting autumn. Autumn is the season associated with the Air Element.

What does it mean? It means in the fields, much of the produce has been harvested, most fruits have been picked. People gather blackberries from the hedgerows; swarms of birds feast on wild berries.

This gathering is significant for the autumn and it is significant for people on many levels, it's a characteristic not only of Autumn but of the Air-element. How come? It seems that the same types of energy that we observe in nature are playing in people's lives and the Element "playing gathering" we call air. We have to re-learn to see ourselves as part of Nature; becoming aware of the elemental energies in nature, means becoming aware of the elemental energies in us. The same play, just different actors!

In terms of people it means: A person, in his/her later stage of life, is said to be in the autumn of life. He or she has gathered much of the fruits of life, may they be children, grandchildren, books, paintings, photos, letters, knowledge or even wisdom. They might have even gathered friends…Hm? Yes recently I learned, that people gather friends on the internet: they call it Face Book - a book of faces, because often the "friend" is just another face. How much do we really know about these "friends" that we collect, like wind collects so many leaves…a play of the Air-energy? It is interesting to note that in the classical systems, Air is also the element of communication. It's through Air that the waves are transmitted to wireless, radio, satellite and mobile phone. Air allows the illusion of being connected…it's a way of replacing "real connections"… for many such connections lessen the sense of separation. The more friends, the more connected; "I live in this technological world; so I gather friends on-line!"

What happens when "gathering" happens?

Go back to watching people gathering berries, they pick some of the berries, those that look ripe and juicy go in the bowl or in the mouth others remain on the bush. Birds do the same.

The wind does the same! How?

On a windy autumn day the wind gathers leaves, dust, seed-pods and petals then carries it for a little distance, and as it hits an obstacle, be it a tree, a fence or wall it drops the leaves and continues on its way. It gathers and lets go; a natural expression of the constant movement of Air. This process of "gathering" on a closer look includes a natural process of selection, selecting that which is useful, the other is left behind. What we gather (collect) appears to us as specially beautiful and useful; this choice is subjective. The trees gathers their sap inwards, withdrawing to their centre – for the sap , the life-giving force is more important than the expressions (leaves) which can be "left behind". The bi-product of this separation effect is an amazingly glorious, beautiful show of colour. The beauty and luminosity of a Vermont or Canadian autumn is legendary, and let's not forget upstate New York or the equally stunning beauty of Japanese mountain-scapes at this time of the year.

This process happens not just in nature, but in a person's life. The riches of a person's life might be summoned up at this stage in an array of talents never seen before. People in the autumn of life might reveal insights and visions of great beauty and of great service to others.

Let's be clear, the beauty comes not from the accumulation, from the amassing of things, but from the natural selection, from that which remains when what is not needed is dropped. Back to Air; it gathers not only leaves it gathers vapour, pollutants and dust throughout its existence. (and so do we) But after a while – Air drops these – only pure beautiful, crisp air remains; ultimately pure life-giving energy, prana remains. With that pure air, everything looks sharp, fresh with intense colour, glowing with palatable beauty. Our problem? Where to find such good clean air? Where to find such good clear, pure teachings… (I don't need to remind you of what happened to so called Yoga in recent times). Where do we find wise people who are clear, translucent even and of a radiant inner beauty?

All of these seem rare. Why? Contrary to the wind, we get attached to what we gathered! When air has gathered too many pollutants and cannot drop them - air becomes poison! Thousands suffer from lung-disease because the Air Element is in our time, frequently out of balance! And just as rare as "clean pure air" are people who gathered the fruits of their lives with discrimination, dropping that which is not needed. This is the teaching of renunciation. Select those berries that are perfect for your purpose, not more, not less and leave the rest behind.

Whether Air, wind or people we need to drop what is not needed. But modern life encourages us to collect the third car in a family, the fifth television, the second "Hamburger" of the day, the umpteenth trinket or the thirtieth pair of sneakers. We might even feel superior because we collect jewellery, antiques, art, money or "celebrity friends"…and we don't know that we constantly collect impressions/memories/ in our mind. We gather…but cannot drop that which is hindering our movement forward. We can't drop even the abusive partner. Our Air energy is out of balance. With all the experiences, the habits and opinions we become heavier and heavier and eventually stagnate because we "simply can't move any more". Air knows better!

Air says: Drop it! Leave it behind. Only when you drop can you become clear and move forward to renewal and your ability to serve all life; gather, yes but with discrimination!

There are obvious similarities between phenomena and nature and people. How can it be different, we are nature! The natural expressions out there are the same as the phenomena in here! In Nature, there are cycles, there are phases, it's not always autumn, it's not always spring- there is permanent change. So there are young people (in the phase of spring) yet behaving as though in the "autumn of life" gathering consumer goods unable to let go; and we have elder people who still show their medals or stick to the same old stories gathered "way back then". These are examples of imbalances in the Air-Element.

We like everything else is made up of these Five Great energy fields. And at the time of our arrival in this earthly dimension, we arrive as a mixture of these Five. Any mixture has one ingredient which is more than the others; this determines "the flavour". More flour than nuts and fruits ...makes the mixture to be "bread", more nuts and fruit makes the dough into cake. This dominating flavour, we call our constitutional Element. It determines how we are, in health and sickness and how we relate to other people.

So a person with the "flavour" of Air, will turn out to be someone who mentally and physically finds it easy to move (agile/flexible or move in terms of career, or places, or relationships) in his/her movement; they collect or gathers things (be it property/antique furniture or friends, partners or knowledge!) *In a healthy balanced way this happens with discrimination,* selective in terms of what the goal/purpose requires; but in a pathological way people amass things "they don't need" i.e. the memory of a difficult relationship, or the tenth pair of jeans! Depending on how attached people become to their "Gatherings", these will cloud their perception of reality; it will constipate, soul, mind and body! Meaning, the person who is hanging on to things/being or thoughts/ideas (dogmatism), is really suffering from Constipation!

Physical Constipation is merely an expression of that energy pattern; other expressions are: "holding on for dear life", rather than letting go what is not needed - or inappropriate in the present situation; even "not doing or taking what is not needed". And with that we are right in the *Yamas and Niyamas.* Yes, if everything is manifestation of the five energy fields, than the Yamas and Niyamas too. In the negative energy state of Air, one needs to practice Asteya (non-stealing) and Aparigraha (not desiring) so that the beauty of the clear Air can shine through (Satya and Shauca). In the positive state, the person "flavoured" by the Air Element has a natural tendency to think clearly and to live simply, with a clear goal ahead. They are people who use the intellect to organize, structure and create, be that in commerce, engineering, science, research or even art (constructionism and Reconstructionism).

In the technology orientated world of today, this capacity might express itself in people who have a natural aptitude to work with organisations, be it for humanitarian reasons, management or especially in the world of computing.

In autumn, in Air and in people (flavoured by this energy-field) there is movement (as expression of gathering – and leaving behind), there is withdrawal onto the basic; just as the trees shed their leaves to preserve the sap in the centre we can go back to: Bare Bones (as Zen Buddhism says). One mustn't fall in the trap to think: people under the influence of this energy, are hard (although it could be) or mean (although it could be), loners (although it could be) BUT they are people who know what is important to them and they shun all unnecessary surplus; they are able to focus on what matters to them, their goals, their beliefs, their possessions, their relationships.

Lack of this energy means: people cannot focus, cannot let go of relationships that are out-lived, cannot let go of feelings they harboured since childhood; cannot overcome likes and dislikes, cannot breath evenly and deeply; they drown in their accumulations and never having enough. This "constipation" on many levels shows an imbalance in this energy field, which eventually might manifest in dis-ease and illness of the related organs i.e. Lungs and large Intestines.

The question is what to do to balance? Autumn is one phase of the year, being an elder is one phase of life; balance comes as a natural part of movement. When movement is allowed there is change; cultivating awareness of change is balancing. Nature's permanent change is Life. A person with imbalances here needs to see the bigger picture, the picture of permanent change…or we could say in using Buddhist/Yogic mixed metaphors: "impermanence" is the nature of "Prakriti". Seeing, understanding, studying, using the ability of the Air Element itself - can correct the imbalance (svadhaya/ Jnana Yoga).

Well said, but we are all Five Elements, and "my dominant Element is Earth, I have no interest in study!" Fine, there are other ways: Here comes the importance of Pranayama and of Swara Yoga (working with the breath, to create movement of the energies).
Well and good, "But I have no opportunity for that where I live?"

OK, there are other ways still: practice purification that teaches the body to let go: i.e. Cleansing practices like nasal and stomach washes, fasting, purifying the thoughts by silence practice, etc. Furthermore, there are herbs and foods that help the balancing act. (Consult an Ayurvedic doctor or one trained in TCM (Traditional Chinese Medicine)). Ultimately there is of course no other practice that is more "simple" and always available than: Meditation

We said: **Autumn is embedded in its relationship with summer and winter.** No person lives as an island; we are embedded in relationships with others. If I have a certain dominant Element, then so have you! Our relationships are determined by the mutual influences between these.

What does this mean..? It means the way your relationship with your boss, your children or your partner takes shape- (joys as well as problems) are due to the interaction between you, shaped by one Element- and the other shaped by another dominant element.
Wow! Yes! Logical and amazing! You can go for a walk, contemplate nature and solve the relationship problems you have, by "reading the book of nature"? Yes!

Let's have a simplified look at relationships from this angle:
Look at the relationship between **Air and Earth**. They mainly "touch" along the surface of Earth; from there Air rises, leaving Earth behind; Air moves over the Earth without much involvement, despite the fact that Earth is the originator of Air, much like the relationship between mother and child. Once a child has grown up there is little interaction. Similarly Air glides over Earth with little interaction, they live 'parallel lives'. If they both accept this, it is fine; but if one of them demands attention…the issues start. Air

cannot move the Earth; it can merely pick up some "dust on the surface."! And on the other hand, Earth cannot really get in the way of Air, even if Earth puts a mountain in the way of Air, the latter simply ascends to higher realms. If Earth wants to tie down Air - Air will "just go elsewhere".

Furthermore: Lies and deceit do not work in this relationship, clean fresh, sharp Air will immediately detect any dishonesty. On the other hand Air might "dance" all it wants Earth will not stand for it. Only mutual tolerance and honest responses can foster their interaction. However potentially the Air person is seemingly so vast, so powerful, so extensive and elusive, that the solid, contracted, heavy Earth has little chance of 'measuring up', unless it finds its value in a different way, which might be the everyday level of pragmatic, manifest living. The strength and solidity of the "Earth person" can well be a "life-saver for the lofty Air person! Here is the secret for their meaningful relationship; a relationship based on acceptance of their vast difference but with mutual support. This can bring positive interaction and growth beyond mere coexistence.

The relationship between **Air and Water** appears similar, as air appears to glide over water, just like over earth. After all, water covers most of the planet earth. It is said that the wave-patterns of the seas are due to the Air movements, yet even that is only surface interaction. Yet there is great difference Air/Oxygen penetrates quite deep into the Water…in fact it is part of its 'make–up' (H^2O). That points to a close, sharing relationship which can even have its passionate moments (foam). Air- and Water-people like to spend time and space together, and enjoy each other. Problems arise in their relationship mainly for two reasons: in the highest spheres (or the desert) air exists with hardly any water. Furthermore if air gets too saturated with water (clouds) i.e. it gets too heavy, it lets go of water (rain). So independence sits well with Air, she is quiet happy to do "her thing" and when things get too heavy, or "she" moves too fast, water gets dropped; Air gets scared of being slowed down. In a relationship, this can mean quite literally – the Air-person moves out of the home or environment. If two people sharing these energies want to make their relationship last, they have to work on balancing their act. The Air person needs the Water person to give her space, to stay fresh, moist and not interfering .Stagnant water (stuck in its own issues) is of no use to Air. Air is light, rises upwards; water has the tendency to sink into the depths; be this is physically or psychologically. Unless they limit themselves, they end up in opposite directionss.

The relationship between **Air and Fire** is startlingly different. Immediately we are caught up in dynamics. Right from the start Air and Fire work together. Air feels needed even with the tiniest spark of fire; it is only a question of time as to when passion rises. However when it does, Air is consumed by Fire; a burning candle in a jar extinguishes as soon as a lid is put on – and it becomes difficult to open the jar afterwards - why? Because inside is a vacuum left by the consumed air; i.e. both suffer! If allowed, Air fuelling fire creates incredible passionate colourful, warm and loving interactions, yet there is always the danger of ending in annihilation! Therefore moderation and discipline are the keys to such a volatile relationship- yet that is almost asking the impossible from their interaction! A moderate draft on a coal fire provides the comfort of home fires… when we open the chimney flap, fire might burn too fast.

On the other side, these two people have a great time, making each other shine and shimmer. They help each other grow and transform; from that perspective there could be no better partner for Air than a Fire person. Yet for all the stimulus and wonderful varied interaction the Air person must be vigilant that he doesn't lose him/ herself in the passion of the Fire person. He/she must retain some distance, space, integrity, privacy etc. By the grace of inspiration from the Fire person, the Air keeps moving; the Fire person keeps Air entertained, amused, and inspired, on their toes, ready to roll away from gathering dust over yesterday's dreams!

Finally we contemplate the relationship between **Air and the fifth element**. At a first glance we might fall prey to the illusion that space and air are identical; using discrimination we become aware that between me and the window is both space and air. Air fills space so completely it's hard to separate the two, why? Because they share many attributes, (transparent, subtle, movement, potential change, etc. etc.) yet space is so much vaster, and subtler than Air. Air is relative gross/ manifest compared to Space, which has many more dimensions of which only one of them is the gross space we are aware of.

Meaning: the Air person is happy and grateful to share his/ her space with the Space person. S/he is at ease and satisfied and finds security in 'Space' as well as enough initiative and movement to fulfil his/her wants and needs. But - Air is not enough for the Space person to express his/her vast potential and interests. In a relationship between an Air person and a Space person, they would be advised to cultivate and foster other aspects of their personality, so that they do not depend on each other for their needs. The Air person has to learn to let go of the partner enough, so that Space can fulfil its destiny and follow their own interests.

We can explore and learn from these Elements, because all the phenomenal universe is made up of combinations of these five basic ingredients, Indian philosophy calls the “bhutas”, “each of them contains different portions of matter (prakriti) and consciousness (purusha) ....these are neither literally earth, water, fire, air and space , nor merely material molecular substances. They are ‘elemental’ in the sense that everything can be analysed (and understood) into some combination of them...” (Yoga and psychotherapy, Swami Rama, R, Ballentine, Swami Ajaya; p. 180...)

Space, its season and relationships

Have you ever wondered what Space actually is? You might think: of course we know! It is the distance or the relationship between objects, between you and me, between the stars and the earth – between one universe and the next!

Hm…Yes but what is it, that is in between? If we start to look into this question, it seems that there are many theories.
1) Space is that substance which carries light and sound waves…. these are essentially electromagnetic waves; which as a field are self-sustaining carriers…so Space itself has no substance , yet it carries electromagnetic or (electro-dynamic) waves- which gives it "substance".
2) Space is electromagnetic waves which carry light….some say - these are light. Does this mean Space and light are the same?
3) These electromagnetic waves also cause sound…making light, sound and space the same?
4) It is said that Space is suffused with quantum fields and possibly with a form of energy called "cosmological constant"; which until recently was called "ether"; what is that?
5) Some say Space is a cosmological hologram, that reflects emptiness; …yet Space as emptiness "holds all potential of creation" surely rendering talk about emptiness meaningless.
6) If, then Space is potentiality (Quantum physics) an ocean of energies; (i.e. Higgs field, a field created by High Energy Collisions), it makes Space teeming with quantum activity of un-manifest potential?
7) Others like Henry Moore fill Space with divine presence; close to what Yogis mean when they say: consciousness-space (chidakasha) being on the subtlest level "*emptiness filled with*

formless consciousness".

So really we don't know what Space is, however we can describe what role it plays in phenomenal existence. It holds "formless consciousness (knowing itself) ; it holds the matrix, the eternal laws according to which all planets move, according to which all life moves; it expands and contracts - in tune with the pulse of creation. These laws keep harmony planets do not collide and lettuces don't grow cherries. Each part of creation has a unique blueprint / *dharma* according to which unfolding happens according to certain (cosmic laws), withholding nothing.

There is a beautiful story about the Indian God Indra, the greatest of the Hindu pantheon. It tells about Indra and his battle with Vritra, "the one that resists and withholds". Vritra takes on the form of a cloud and holds back the life giving rains. It resulted in gloom and doom on the earth, there was only depression, sadness and darkness; there was no growth neither of plants nor human life. Indra decided to help the world. He drank three lakes of nectar, and thus armed, tackled Vritra, striking him with a thunderbolt in his back and in his face with a pointed dagger. When he had killed the demon, water burst from the clouds and from springs on earth and immediately growth started, the plains and fields started to bloom everywhere, trees started to sprout, light and joy was there again accompanying life and growth.

Withholding, as can be seen is the greatest enemy of growth. In fact its death,...as we know it. There is a tradition in Yoga which says, that holding the breath...is a little death , hence it is advocated to breath slowly and continuously, providing permanent even supply of prana (life-energy). To withhold...is not giving; to give i.e. give seva, self-less service, even sacrifice is the core-law of the cosmos. Giving freely, giving generously and not withhold anything, is one way to ensure smooth unfolding played out in Space.

However, regular even expansion is rare in human terms. We usually breathe and act erratic: things happen we react (frequently not very appropriately). Life's influences come, distort our pattens and imbalances appear, instead of watching this play - we get involved! Why? Because we lose sight of the overall picture, we lose our sense of balance, the rising sap gets blocked and frustration and anger distorts our being.

The cosmic laws that are inherent in Space ensure balanced existence. From Space (the subtlest of the Elements in yogic understanding) comes the gross (all phenomenal existence); thus **Space energy is creativity par excellence;** for this all other elements are roped in – all others serve Space; they help with its job of creation. Sankhya says... the purpose of everything is to serve... gross Elements then serve the subtle Elements, ultimately serve subtlest Space, and beyond.

Let's look at an example how all Elements partake in the action of creation: to create a picture we take the canvas (Earth) paint (Water) the idea (Fire) the intelligent movement of the brush (Air). Similarly we take pen and paper, ink, ideas and words and create a poem or write a book. We take food, water, thoughts, feelings and impressions and constantly create ourselves. All that is alive partakes in this process, constantly procreating or co-creating. **All existence comes from this creativity inherent in Space; hence Space is associated with Spring.**

In some countries… spring summer winter autumn are all seasons that merge into each other… and that two befits the character of Space, as it holds all Elements; but in the temperate Zones of our globe, spring is the most creative time, where the period of rest, of hibernation, of withdrawal is over and life seems to spring forth everywhere. Seeds sprout, trees bloom, earth breaks open to reveal carpets of flowers….

I have talked frequently about Cornwall, the location where I lived; the word Cornwall comes from Cerwidden, the Celtic name for the Goddess of Spring! Spring there lasts for 4 months; already in February, the grounds are covered with snowdrops (white spring flowers), from December yellow daffodils can be seen in gardens, eventually covering fields, road sides and even cliffs right down to the sea, followed by bluebells, camellias, rhododendrons and the most enormous magnolia trees, with flowers as big as a child's head.

Spring is time of exceptionally prolific "bringing forth"; a time displaying the power of the Creatrix…the Great Mother, creative life-energy per se. When, in a human being this very energy is disturbed, when the urge to create itself gets blocked - illnesses and suffering is the result on the manifest level. Life –force is creative per se…throughout the cosmos, throughout 'Space"…including us, when that drive is frustrated not beauty but pain results. Just think of the mental pain, infertility brings to a couple desiring a child; or the mental agony and dissatisfaction over spoilt plans for a certain lifestyle. Think of the resulting irritability because 'I cannot go to a certain concert because I lack the money', or the irritation of not finding the right words to express oneself, or the impatience that one's arthritic joints will not allow one to go 'just anywhere.'

We can observe these distortions in the posture of a person with a dominant element of Space; the frustration makes the whole being look as though he is imprisoned in his own body. He or she will look inflexible, with stiff legs and a 'wooden gait.' However, if the person is not just frustrated, but simply lacks the energy of the Space Element there seems nothing holding him or her up; the body seems floppy and it might even oscillate from side to side; such people might not to be able to walk in a straight line; they always bump into other people. A lack of this energy, gives a lack of purpose, such people might feel without direction in life. This road seems just as attractive as that; this partner just as attractive as that one. If there is no preference - where to go? Choice becomes a nightmare, causing confusion – rendering the person not only ambivalent but ineffectual.

Sometimes one can recognise problems in gestures that people themselves often are unaware of. In the above case, we might observe a habit of holding the head at an angle… (which way to look at things?); their feet might be unsure where to go; there hands might dangle purposelessly beside their body, without strength; if we look at their shoes, they might be worn at the outside rim (body weight being placed in a way that shows no core-stability) etc. etc.

However what can we do to redress any imbalances in the Space-energy-field? It must be mentioned that of course therapies such as Acupuncture, Shiatsu, Kinesiology etc. – any therapy that works on balancing energies…helps! But the very character of a Space- person makes them more inclined to help him/herself. Having a larger perspective than most, Space –people might be able to 'see the problem' and look for 'a plan' to put things right.

As this energy field is connected to tendons and ligaments which make movement possible, one obvious help comes from doing exercises, that might be simply walking , practicing Hatha Yoga, Martial arts, Qi Quong, Tai Chi etc. or any form of Self-Healing. It gives them the feeling of 'doing something' and being in 'control.' Self help books fill the shelves of bookshops. This ever-increasing, popular industry is though not without danger. Mostly these come from our mind, which will lead us astray; pride, anger and desires colour our analysis - we see what we want to see, we cure what we want to cure! There is nothing wrong with this 'placebo-effect', but the danger lies doing the wrong things, for the wrong reasons, for the sake of our ego! Because the Space-person is such visionary, this danger for him/her is probably even more so- than for others.

The Tibetan way of Self-Healing introduced by Lama Gangchen Rinpoche, called *Ngal-So* relaxes body and mind completely; *Ngal* refers to relative truth, while *So* refers to absolute truth; *Ngal* also means darkness, *So* means light (much like the Sanskrit: *Gu-ru*). Here like in all Buddhists thought (just as in Yoga) good health is a matter of creating "a beautiful mind". The healing process thus includes creating positive thoughts and energies through an ancient praxis that integrates colour - and sound - therapy to open blockages using mudras (gestures), syllables and symbols, as well as visualizations and breathing. These are essentially tantric practices, which of course we also can find in the wider yogic context.

Food is of course, specifically beneficial for balancing the Space/Wood (in Chinese). It should be chosen for its ability to help distribute nutrients and blood, to activate and circulate *Qi* (Samana Prana) and for its ability to replenish blood and moisture. So food with a stimulating as well as enriching character, such as sweet, sour, juicy and astringent food, is looked for. Nuts such as pine nuts, almonds, sesame and chestnuts are recommended. Honey is advised as a sweetener; vegetables are suggested such as leeks, carrots, spinach, beets, Chinese cabbage and watercress; fruits such as dates, cherries, blackberries and strawberries are recommended, as well as apples, pears, bananas, olives etc.; and of course all manner of beans, rice etc. It is as well to keep in mind that foods should be chosen carefully, in accordance with the season, and within the latitude in which one lives, yet much more detailed advice is needed than can be given here.

As the concept of homeopathy teaches us - like can be cured with like, thus if t**he imbalances of Space energy arises out of frustrated creativity, it might be healed by freeing creative energy,** letting it flow into another branch, another direction: find new and different ways of being creative; dance, paint, start working with clay, write poems or learn creative cooking…Channelling the creative energy might have amazing effects as we know from stories where a couple tried in vain to have a child, but as soon as they have adopted a child, the mother gets pregnant; life energy is freed. To become creative is a truly profound way to free Space energy, but let us go even deeper. Spaces creativity is merely an unfolding of what is inherent, that means discovering one's purpose one's dharma and removing that which stops the unfoldment of this inherent purpose. To live according to one's *dharma* automatically will lead to living. The acorn has the potential of the tree, when nothing is put in its way it will become an oak tree. It is not what we add to life that is important, but what we don't add! **Contemplating this reveals that Space energy can be balanced simply by living the right *dharma*.** It is easy to see the *dharma* of the acorn, 'the tree is treeing'; to search for the purpose of our life and live it… is balancing; is balancing Space energy. Once we are established in this awareness and live in it, with total integrity, the highest potential of every living Being unfolds; it is the legacy of Space that propels us beyond even Space.

And here we come across another aspect of Space we have so far neglected here. **Space has two aspects; physical Space and consciousness space.** In short imbalances in our lives can also be caused because we pay no attention to that subtler Space, i.e. our spiritual dimension. **If we neglect our spiritual calling, our path…we will not find the answer to "what am I here for".** The question needs ultimately be answered in a wider context… or we could say: a subtler context; from an inner vision, inner wisdom through contemplation will reveal the answers. In the stillness of meditation you will find solutions. This very silence of the mind will avoid being fooled by your mind, i.e. producing 'wild, useless shoots.'

Become a witness of the activities of your own mind and body; observe and take charge of your life. **Nothing is an accident; we experience what we need to experience,** the Divine will carries us into a certain direction. Be alert and awake to hear that call. This practice will lay down the fear of having wasted your life and save you from the ultimate frustration of being helpless in acting out your true purpose.

Once the quest has revealed what we need to know, then we need to act upon it, and that involves others; we cannot stay in contemplation forever and withhold our energy, it has to be shared. Just as a true painter does not just paint pictures secretly in a back room, but has the pictures shown to others, exhibited, vented under the public eye, and eventually let go, sold. Music has not just to be written down, or heard in one's own ears, but to be played with instruments, performed in concerts etc.

We are all familiar with the painted faces of American Indians;

they were originally not primarily to frighten the enemy, or even less to hide behind; no, quite the opposite. The painted faces used in ceremonies as well as wars were showing the beauty and the achievement, the identity of the individual soul. The design and colour was chosen to express the individual's inner truth, or medicine. The painted face is a way of self-expression. It is an expression of whom and what the wearer truly is - not what we on the outside perceive him to be. It allows others to see, and in a way opens up their reactions to the truth of the wearer; who offers his real Self to be relied on, to be used by others.

A Space-person is a person with vision, full of potential ideas, concepts and castles. They are highly imaginative and have a quick mind that is not bothered about details, daily routines and accounting, but they are free, at least in spirit. They can 'fly.' They look at the overall usefulness of a plan; they sum up a whole theory in a few words at a board meeting! They might 'direct armies,' or use their ability to influence the course of humanity. Their life is not to be limited by pettiness, by withdrawal into safe niches, a cosy family or individual concerns – at best they live for the betterment of humanity. Such people have foresight, they see the consequences of actions before they happen; they learn lessons from past failures; they see the wisdom of the ancestors and respond.

They can see for example what calamities the long-term use of chemicals causes; they can see how misuse of Earth's resources will affect the future generations! Their task is to protect the children and the future children! The American Indians say you shall not do anything that adversely affects the children of the seventh generation! That is thinking from the point of Space.

Such people have the ability to foresee present and future needs and trends and thus the survival of a company, the wellbeing of a nation, even the survival of the human race is in safe hands with them. Such an extraordinary person has not only the ability 'to fly him/herself' but to do so for the good of all!

A vital point needs to be made here! The extraordinary Space person can 'fly high' because he/she has made the 'ultimate sacrifice' - given up self-interest! Space just is, it contains all other elements having no more 'individual little niches' for himself. A person of such calibre, having given up the ego, acts from a total different level than the other elements. **Space can 'fly high' precisely because of having given up 'being manifest earth; nurturing water; transforming fire and life-providing air.'** Such a person is the rarest indeed, the most highly evolved amongst human beings! However because her overall vision... she easily breaks traditions, family ties and conventions - she needs to be free. She inspires others with her confidence, ambitions and dreams; she knows she can overcome all obstacles.

However knock-backs do happen, especially when she out-distances people. They cannot follow her many flights and high standards. So how does she relate to the others? How does the

Space-person relate to the Earth-person? Space is above, around and in Earth; Earth exists within her, like a fish exists in water; there is an intimate connection. However Space doesn't hold Earth tight; it allows earth to float unencumbered within the limits of its orbit. Space does not force Earth to do anything; it allows Earth to do its own thing. Space is limitless - Earth is bound by its own gravity, solid and staid. These two seem light-years apart from each other, making it difficult for Space to understand Earth. Space simply accepts that Earth is OK in its own, particular way. This detached relationship benefits when both explore their inner nature; Space respects Earth for being one of its finest creations; Earth gains inspiration, realising that space is part of each of its particles. With this awareness they meet in 'sacred, Space.' How would a relationship between two such different people be? On the earthly plane, they could benefit from each other: one from the grounding effect of the other; one from the freeing and expanding way of the former. Space in its abstract and limitless nature, needs the confines and solidity of Earth to make its many ideas manifest, just as much as Earth needs the door to more freedom, which Space can provide.

How does **Space relate to Water?** Space allows Water, with its fluid nature to follow it; where they meet, they have a very close relationship, operating in the same dimension and time. They fit hand in glove; Space leads and Water follows like a pair of classic Ballroom dancers. As soon as Space has a new idea, a new concept, Water follows suit, taking on the idea and feeding it and making it bloom. As long as Water can keep following, there is no discord - but... there is no water in 'outer space!' Meaning: Conflict arises when the Space person is tempted to loftier heights where 'nobody' can follow not even water!

How does **Space relate with Fire**? There is much to contemplate; here are only a few pointers: 'Fire' as in the suns, moons, stars and planets are strewn throughout space; they follow much of their own path within cosmic space. In our world, space contains equally the three forms of fire, and there is no difference to Space whether the sun shines, flames hungrily devour and transform much of space's creation, or the warmth of a hearth fire is attended or left to die!

Again, Space is characterised by two aspects; all activity happens within it -yet it is not involved. The two come together when Krishna talks to Arjuna in the Bhagavad Gita about detachment; it does not mean not acting - but being detached from the fruit resulting from the action.

In a relationship between a person characterised by the element of Space and a partner characterised by Fire, there is lively and passionate interaction. As long as Space stays calm in the background, uninvolved, letting the Fire person take the centre of the stage - the Fire person can create a universe; she can live a flamboyant, active life. Trouble starts when the Space person does not remain in the back ground, but wakes up, is in his active creative, driving role. Then the two will have much conflict; they will be like warriors invading each other's territory, and eventually destroying each other with their inherent fire, passion and anger. A relationship between these depends on the intensity of their tendencies and the ability of Space (Wood) to be detached! Space cannot solve the conflict with Fire by entering into battle, but by being creative and with that, giving Fire fuel to unfold.

We move on to the last element with which **Space interacts, Air.** From the vantage-point of Space, space and air are almost too close! On our planet one could be tempted to think, that where there is space, there is air. In fact air dissolves into space in the higher spheres. As far as we know, life-sustaining air though is only wrapped around earth and no other planets. For space in its cosmic regions, air is merely one of many substances it holds and thus space by and large, is not too bothered about this rival. Only once we look closer to the ground, does the rivalry seem to matter.

The relationship between Space - and Air seems to have two aspects; they are almost identical yet with this very fact they are prone to injure each other. How? By reinforcing the same tendencies. Both Air and Space can escape; becoming aloof and uninvolved – they dry up, retreat into isolation. It's a fine line- where such detached focus becomes saintly – or mad.

However in every-day life we could find just as well that the opposite is true; for example: that Space unaware of its grand purpose, gets glued and lives in symbiosis with earth, water, fire, and air. Due to this close symbiosis, Space-people are in danger at times, to forget that they are also the space beyond; Space needs to remember that she is the stage on which the others play! True to her dharma, she needs to explore her grounded-ness (in the manifest earth) and her limitlessness; spanning a wide vision; such is the nature of a Boddhisattva; a Buddha that after enlightenment decides to 'go back to the market place' and help others in this world to find their way.

Space- and Air persons in their ideal state both have unlimited ability to gather knowledge and wisdom; which might lead to great understanding for each other- but could also lead to rivalry and even envy and resentment , especially if one stops the other from reaching their potential. In such a case, Space then might simply step out and do his/her own thing; especially when Space's vision and freedom is threatened by Air's tendency to be dogmatic.

Potentially each **Element also relates to people, that are like him/herself** dominated in character by the same element. These meetings will be either like looking in a mirror, or showing a different facet of the same element. There are countless variations of the theme. But let's just have the briefest, simplistic preview.

Assuming that an **Earth person meets another Earth person,** both are reliable, hold and support others. They would feel like sisters/brothers. However, if one of them is characterised by a negative Earth state, being egocentric, unreliable and totally absorbed into their own health, possessions, body, interests, etc., rock hard and with total lack of compassion, sympathy or interest in others, such an Earth person might feel less than a sister, and more like an alien.

A Water person in relationship with a Water person, might be mutually supportive, nourishing, and be great companions. If you add water to water, it is as one. Due to its ability to feel into others, a Water person might even be safe enough to be able to feel into the dark sides of their own character. In this way, even a companion that shows a totally different aspect e.g. ice or vapour, would still find empathy and understanding; because of water's adaptability and flexibility, there could always be shared interest.

As for **Fire meeting another Fire person**, who knows? They could increase each other's flame and enthusiastically share their ideas and spur each other on, albeit if the fires get too big, they would starve each other of the much needed oxygen and destroy each other. Two closely involved Fire people are unlikely to last long.

As for **two Air people relating** with each other? Can you add air to air? If you do, they share existence with little change; neither enriching - nor taking from each other. Air and air just lose themselves into each other. This might be a relationship without challenge, stimulus - and without tension, simply two people beating with one heart.

Two Space people? Well you cannot add space to space. A relationship between two Space people is a relationship with unlimited creativity and noble aspirations; they would work together onto some greater cause to serve the world. The idea of spiritual communities where people help each other to strive for the highest has meaning here, as has the relationship between Guru and disciple, between teacher and student. Young trees flourish in mutual support and protection - each one to their own karma. Thus dharma will grow; some will grow taller than others, yet all will evolve.

Our responsibility towards the Great Five

We are our teeth, our skin, our hands, our feet our organs. We take care of them. We unquestionable brush our teeth at least twice a day; we put all sorts of creams and oils on our skin to keep it healthy, we look after our feet, our hands by cutting our nails and putting lotions on our limbs. We look after our health by eating properly and if something does not feel right we go to the doctor to "make things better".

We are the Five Elements; the body of the Earth, our Mother, is the Five Elements. What do we do to keep those healthy? In fact we violate them from dawn to dusk. I remember reading an alarming question: would you stub out your cigarette on your mothers skin? Would you tar the skin of your mother, would you ask your mother to inhale exhaust fumes? Yet that's what we do to our Earth-mother. In fact our entire modern world seems to be built on mistreating the Elements. We recognize our responsibility towards our body, but do not recognize the responsibility towards the Elements. How can we be so negligent? Because we have forgotten that we are the Elements, we are part of Nature.

In ancient times, man new himself embedded in the general cosmos. In fact, the cosmos itself was often depicted as a Being and all that happened in it, was likened to what happens in a human body. According to that imagery: we humans are like so many blood-cells in the cosmic body… all doing their job, **for the greater good** of the body. Now for a while human civilization has not behaved accordingly, but has done what it individually wants!

Staying in the imagery of the cosmic body, man has behaved as a blood-cell, which "does its own thing". If this happens in a human

body ....we call it Cancer!
As human beings we have disregarded the "Greater Good" and behaved like Cancer cells; forgetting to live and work in harmony with All existence.

The deepest tragedy of our age is that we humans have forgotten our place in the universe; we have forgotten who we are, and think that we are in charge of life, that our individual small little egos can do what it wants; it means we talk only about a fraction of ourselves. **We only think and act from one aspect of our existence, the conditioned Ego – I.** We forget that we, like the entire known world are linked and their existence is an unfolding of the Five Elements, five different energy-fields. And within that, human existence is simply one smallest entity. And yet this small unimportant form of existence, that can be squashed by the earth in a simple little shake....thinks it's all important, and the entire creation is for its egoistic use. How stupid are we, how limited our thinking, how great our foolishness?

It's the old story of the sorcerer's apprentice! We seem to know better than the Master; whatever we call HIM. How can the small self, have this illusion? Only because it's thinking is so limited that it sees itself as separate as autonomous, as big important individual "I"! Who has dominion over Nature! It forgets its source and interdependence with the rest of existence.

We need to wake-up to the fact, that we are Nature, not part of it. Just like your hands or your teeth are you...not separate entities! And that means just as we need to look after our teeth... or we will suffer, we have to look after nature or we will suffer. And that is the state of our globe; at present; 2/3 thirds of the population suffer because of our greed; and scientists of all manner of disciplines, tell us, that we have neglected the Elements almost beyond recovery. We are bent on self-destruction.

The main tenet of Yogic ethics is Ahimsa. Non-harming, what does it mean? It certainly doesn't just mean "do not kill" and although it is almost part of any moral code... we still do plenty of it.

We inflict harm and injury, with words, with glances, with all manner of actions – including the most violent forms of killing. We kill by robbing each-other of clean drinking water; of clean air to breath...we kill animals and all manner of species at an alarming rate, by cutting down their habitats or polluting the ocean...for what? So we can take a cruise as a holiday. We don't even realise that today's great ocean-liners are one of the main destroyers of marine life!

Why all this destruction? **Because of our ever growing greed and because of our ignorant minds, that forget that we live in a world where everything is connected with everything else.**

Have you ever contemplated your simple act of having a nice cup of tea, in your home...and what it means:
Someone in Darjeeling had to pick the tea-leaves, dry them and pack them. Not only does the life of the pickers and their children depend on the price of tea we pay, but their grandparent's work of preparing the land, planting and nurturing the bushes connects them too to your cup of tea. Only because of their hard labour you can enjoy your tea...but you deprive their children of enough income to go to school.

We forget our gratitude towards Mother Nature; earth, air, sun and the rain have been given just in the right measure so that the tea could grow for our pleasure.

Once harvested, the tea had to be shipped; oil had to be bought for the ship's engines and various lorries for transport. Many people contributed and handled the tea until it finally ended up on the supermarket shelf. And there too staff were involved; the cashier and even the bus driver who brought you home etc. Thousands of people, several countries, and all of nature are involved in your simple 'cup of tea' – And more over how many of them suffered in the process?

The tea-bush…makes its new leaves…but before they unfold… they are broken, life snapped from them…they suffer. As we mentioned before: we pay too low prices for tea…hence the children of the pickers in Sri Lanka do not get enough food or schooling. The shopkeepers or lorry drivers that bring the tea to your shop are deprived of sleep…have to work inhumanly long hours to make a living…they suffer...............And so on, and on….

Everything connected to anything else, so what we do to other people, what we do to the Earth, the Waters, the Fire, the Air and even Space affects all of us and more than that, future generations. We have polluted the earth, by putting atomic waste inside mountains! Buried Plutonium in cliffs and under seabeds…. In other words inside Mother Earth!

We have polluted the oceans, so that fish die at an alarming rate, and the sea is full of plastic particles left over from our industry and waste products such as cans that will take 500 years to decompose. There are whole areas of the ocean which are no more blue waters, but floating garbage basins (as of the coast of Alaska and in the Doldrums). Our rivers are poisoned with chemicals that effect wildlife on an enormous scale. The fish that are in it, are frequently poisoned by heavy metal such as mercury; and full of hormones (leftovers from contraceptive pills make fish and humans alarmingly infertile).

We have exploited the fossil fuels from the bowels of the earth (oil and gas); burned the ancient woods of large areas in South America and Asia, which include medicinal plants that can cure major diseases; and moreover we are killing the environment for people who have ancient knowledge of healing plants. So we cut the lungs of our planet…and erase the very people who would be able to cure the resulting illnesses. For what? To have vast areas of grazing-land for cattle, because we "want to eat meat"; even though we know, that these very cattle are a major contributor to global warming. "Half the world's greenhouse gases are emitted by life-stock" (Grace Shoemaker-Galloway; Nov. 2009) Making cow emission more damaging than cars, planes and factories. The United Nations Food and Agriculture put the gas emission from cows at 18 % of our air-pollution in 2006; it has now reached 51 % as billions of cattle contribute (with chickens not far behind).
How suicidal can humanity become?

We know from our bodies, if we neglect our lungs. .. (the energy and organ-network in our bodies related to the Air-Element) we get all sorts of disease, which eventually might even lead to a pre-mature death. And yet we neglect the lungs of our Earth, the great forests and cut down vast areas of ancient forests. The US is responsible for more greenhouse gas pollution than South America,

Africa, Middle East and Asia altogether (National Geographic Magazine 2010); and yet we blame China and India.

Furthermore we have misused energy to such an extent that we have to feed our greed (Fire) with atomic energy, which pollutes our very earth for millennia. A materialistic society, we are of the nature of Fire Element, we devour, we burn … (The Dagara of West Africa, who describe their world, society, aesthetics, judiciary etc. with the Element concept, describe whole civilizations and cultures in terms of how they are in this world. (re: Malidoma Somé))
We have managed even to pollute Space; there is much debris floating in outer space that there is danger of collision of these garbage heaps in the sky, having a "fallout effect" on Earth.

What will it take to wake us up, to the Truth, that we are not taking responsibility for the Elements, for Life, for our Globe, the finest manifestation of Mother Nature?

There are in the many traditions that work with the Elements, several recognized cycles of interaction; that work for mutual balance; because of these laws our world has flourished.

There is in the Indian Tradition (and others) a cycle of Creation and dissolution; Space, Air, Fire, Water, Earth – Water, Fire, Air Space. We have met this sequence in the above.

It shows how each Element evolved from a subtler, to ever more gross manifestation; when the elements get out of balanced; they are controlled (rebalanced) by each other. In this way Space controls Earth; Earth controls Water; Water controls Fire; Fire controls Air. We can easily see why (example: if Water has no boundaries it goes all over the place, due to its flexibility; Earth controls that by providing river-banks and beaches, cliffs to the ocean…etc.)

There is furthermore a cycle of support, (especially in the Chinese systems) where Space supports Fire, supports Earth, supports Air, supports Water, supports Space. Once we learn how to read the book of nature, we can see these principals at work, and how they keep the Movement of life in balance, be it in our body or in Nature at large.

If we have imbalance, a block a damage in one it effects all others…If the Water-energy is blocked and can't do its job of nurturing, of purifying then it is easy to see how our body will wither and our kidneys will be effected, and eventually the Liver will be effected (Space)…the circulation of blood and the heart will be effected (Fire) which will damage the Lungs (Air) and the body cannot be maintained, (Earth) and the person will die!

It is easy to see if one of the elements is blocked in its function, whether it is that of support or control or generation… all others are effected. Now we live in times where Earth is polluted, (buried heavy metals, that will take tens of thousands years to be "cleaned"); where the Water is getting scarce and polluted (Oceans and rivers), where the Air is polluted (greenhouse gases) and where the fossil energies are used up. What chances do we have, what chance do sentient beings have, to live a life of beauty, health and balance (peace) when every one of these energies, that make up existence are defiled, blocked threatened?

We know this, we read it in the papers, the books, there is no dearth of information about it – it changes nothing! The important question is: how can we take responsibility for the Elements?

There are some great examples. The Tibetan Healer Tulku T.Y.S. Lama Gangchen Rinpoche, travels tirelessly healing people and the environment; especially through his world Peace Foundation. Rinpoche has gathered the wisdom of healing practices for the environment, just as the healing practices for the body. We know manifestation happens from gross to subtle; hence healing starts on a subtle level (www.lgpt.net).

We can learn practices to heal the environment.

There is the Council of thirteen indigenous grandmothers from around the globe, (woman from the Amazon forests, the Tibetan Plateau, the core of Africa and the islands of New Zealand) who tirelessly travel to perform ritual, prayer and meditation to purify our Earth in all its aspect; we can support and connect with these and help to restore a balance of peace. (www.grandmotherscouncil.com). If this is too subtle for you, there are many organisations we can join that work on campaigning… educating people or simply at "collecting litter on the beaches".

BUT more than anything else we have to work on ourselves, to connect with our awareness of nature, with the awareness of how our mental patterns are collectively responsible for creating so much greed and desire that we destroy each other and our very existence. It is our very own minds we have to change; permanent change can only come from that.

Swami Veda Bharati, Sept. 2009; in a meeting of Scientists and Sages "the Power of One" -said in his speech: "The beginning point of all social change and the ending point of all social change is in oneself.

So integrating it all into oneself and daily giving oneself some time for contemplating these issues – not on how to bring change in the society, or how to bring change in the economics, or how to bring change in the social structures of education – but where to bring change in oneself."

We need to ask ourselves: "Where is my level of greed that I can reduce? Where is my level of want that I can reduce? At what level is my peace of mind, that is, absence of conflicts in my mind? And perhaps I have fewer conflicts now than I had ten years ago, but what are those conflicts whose energy needs to be integrated and harmonised, and how do I go about doing it?

Spend time on oneself and *then* be a leader. A good leader is he or she who leads without letting anyone feel that he or she is leading – just by mere presence. A real peacemaker is one who by his or her mere presence generates peace in the surrounding minds.

When we have worked enough on ourselves in this way, spending some time in contemplation and meditation, moments of that silence then bring peace and harmony around us, and the sense of unity around us will expand in concentric circles like a wave spreading out and becoming subtler and subtler and subtler – its energy spreading and in this way similarly forming ten thousand waves.

Yes we need to become involved and active for taking care of the Elements, of the environment and our self in an unprecedented scale; but our motivation, our attitude, our minds from which to do it, have to become purified first....otherwise... we will simply work on "solutions that replace one problem with another", because the root cause, our feeling of separation from nature; our selfish greed and our ego- importance has not been dealt with.

Meaning: Our Fire needs to be balanced with the Water energy, with calm, cool minds that have one aim only that is to nurture, care and love each other as well as all of existence.

Meaning: Our Earth energy of holding on to me and mine has to be balanced by the awareness of Space, of the one spirit that is shared by all existence. We need to be inclusive, not exclusive!

Meaning: Our Water energy needs to be cleaned, the Earth is a great filter and the most effective recycling plant, however we earthlings have to learn not to pollute the waters with all manner of substances, from chemicals to unbalanced microorganisms.

Meaning: Our Air energy needs to be allowed to heal by increasing clean energy- sources like solar energy, wind and sea generated energy (neither fossil fuels nor atomic energy is the answer) .

Meaning: our Space energy needs balancing by keeping outer and inner space free and calm so that prana, the life-force can flow unhindered and unfold according to its timeless dharma.

Hari ohm Tat Sat

About the Author

Swami Nityamuktananda, Dr. Christa-Maria Herrmann (PhD; MA; MEd; DAD; Dip theol; Dip Ed; etc.), German by birth (1945), naturalized British, originally studied Theology; her university studies soon expanded to Education,Psychology, Philosophy and Art and Design (Ceramics). In fact she never stops studying and never stops teaching. Be it in colleges and universities; in workshops and international conferences, in Yoga Institutes and ashrams; or even on Silent Retreats etc. At the centre of her studies and teachings always is the subject of 'Self-awareness'.

Life in Asia (Australia and America) awakened her interest in Eastern Philosophy (Taoism and Zen) and led to the Zen-arts of Raku (as an artist potter she exhibited worldwide) and Shiatsu (one of several complementary medicines she studied and practiced).

She took samnyasa (becoming a traditional Indian renunciate and teacher) in 2003 from Swami Anubhavananda and confirmed her vows in a traditional Vedic ceremony with Swami Veda Bharati in 2007.

As artist and philosopher merged more and more, a unique combination emerged of deep involvement in Meditation, Sattipahana (mindfulness) and Ngal So; as well as the contemplative practices of Jnana Yoga and Vedanta. Throughout, she worked with several great spiritual Masters among them Zen-Masters, great Siddhas, the Tibetan Lama and Tulku T.Y.S. Gangchen, the great Yogi Swami

Maheshananda and H.H. Swami Anubhavananda (Acharya of Vedanta) and M.M. (Mahamadeleschwara) Swami Veda Bharati, disciple of Swami Rama of the Himalayas.

In 1997 she made her Doctorate in Eco-philosophy on the subjects of the Mahabhutas (Five Great Elements) and since then contributes world-wide in conferences and workshop. The wisdom of the universal concept of the Mahabhutas, the five Elements, is a universal concept shared by many, if not all wisdom-traditions around the globe; including but by no means only, Yoga Philosophy.

Swami Nityamuktananda continuously travels around the world, teaching on innumerable topics related to Ethics, Yoga philosophy (incl. Meditation) and "The Five Elements" and this from Norway to New Zealand, from Germany to Mexico; from Japan to Ecuador; from Singapore and Australia to Ireland.

She has been teaching especially in two centres in India, for many years: Kaivalyadhama, Yoga Research Institute, Lonavla as well as SRSG (Swami Rama Sadhaka Grama; Rishikesh Himalayas).

In 1997 she was awarded a 'World-Peace Prize' for contributions to World Peace (LGWPF/ NGO of UN). She is the author of several books (especially an encyclopedic book on the Five Elements; as well as a simpler version translated into Italian, Chinese and Hungarian.)

She writes continuously articles for various website, including her own : www.athayoga.info

Her publications include:

-*Renunciation; A Contemplation of Samnyasa then and Now*

- *Tattva Samasa; Sankhya Philosophy in a Nutshell*

- *The Five Great Elements Rediscovered*

- *Dewdrop in Tomorrow's Ocean*

- *Seeing Yoga, a contemplation of the Yoga Sutras*

- *GU-RU, Contemplation of a Sanskrit Hymn*

-*The Way of Raku.*

There are many recordings of her teachings and lectures on DVD and CD...the list is continously growing.

See www.5elementsglobalproductions.com